To Master William Michael

With All My Love

Aunt Sandi

NURSERY RHYME TOYS

NURSERY RHYME TOYS

By Evelyn Smith

DRAKE PUBLISHERS INC   NEW YORK

IBSN 0–87749–328–6
LCCN 72–12042

Published in 1973 by
Drake Publishers Inc
381 Park Avenue South
New York, N.Y. 10016

Printed in Great Britain

CONTENTS

DEDICATED

to the memory of my husband

FREDERICK SMITH

INTRODUCTION

The toys in this book were designed as groups, each illustrating one of our well-loved nursery rhymes. As such they would be very suitable for a group of people working sociably together, though of course there is no reason why an individual should not tackle any or all of them. They take for granted a knowledge of simple sewing procedures, but do not demand advanced skills.

The materials required are cheap and easily obtainable: Kapok, foam rubber or rayon strands for stuffing; felt, wool, cotton and various odds and ends (often in very small quantities left over from regular dressmaking) for clothes, bodies, features and trimmings.

The toys shown here are only a starting-point, and once you are familiar with the principles of making dolls and their clothes, you will surely be tempted to go on inventing your own.

HEY DIDDLE DIDDLE

Hey diddle diddle, the cat and the fiddle,
The cow jumped over the moon.
The little dog laughed to see such fun,
And the dish ran away with the spoon.

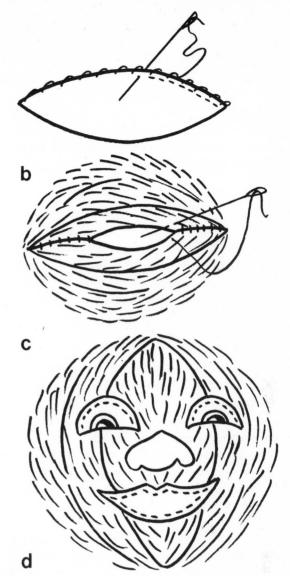

b

c

d

Patterns pp 92–100

MOON   (Washable)

MATERIALS

Lemon fur fabric, 12 in × 26 in (30·5 cm × 66 cm).
Chamois leather, small piece for features.
Foam rubber chippings for fillings.
Blue stranded cotton.
Thread to match fur fabric.

CUT

Eight segments lemon fur fabric, according to pattern; ¼ in (6 mm) turnings are allowed.
Eyes, nose and mouth in chamois leather.

MAKING UP

Take two segments, right sides facing (make sure the pile runs the same way) and with matching thread, starting at A oversew the edges together with stitches ⅛ in (3 mm) apart, finishing at B. Then backstitch ¼ in (6 mm) in from edge (Figs 1a and b). Lay this on one side and continue to join the rest of the segments in couples. Join two couples together in the same way, and finally join one seam of each half moon, and from A to C and B to D on the last seam. This leaves an opening for filling. Turn right side out. Tack a piece of tape along each edge from C to D to stop fraying when filling. Fill fairly firmly with very small pieces of foam rubber. Ladderstitch opening, i.e., take one stitch from one side and one stitch from other side (Fig 1c).

Fig 1

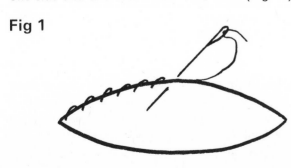

a

Features

Using tiny stitches hem the eyes, nose and mouth in position (Fig 1d). Then with one strand of blue cotton, backstitch the outline of lips and eyes.

COW

MATERIALS

Fur fabric, 18 in × 12 in (46 cm × 30·5 cm). Original used brown and white, but any suitable colour could be used so long as it is short pile.
Felt, scraps of pink, brown and black.
Wire, 16 gauge, one piece 9 in (23 cm) and one piece 7 in (18 cm).
Adhesive tape for binding wire.
Pipe cleaner.
Kapok for filling.
Thread, pink, black and brown.

CUT

Body, underbody, head gusset and two ears in fur fabric, making sure you reverse the pattern to make the pair.

One tail in brown felt.

Two ears, four hoofs, four hoof bases, four horns, one upper lip, one lower lip and two eyes in pink felt.

Two pupils in black felt.

MAKING UP

Body

1. Place one half of underbody to body of cow, right sides facing. Using matching thread, oversew the edges together, with stitches $\frac{1}{8}$ in (3 mm) apart, from A down front leg, under body, and up back leg to B. Now backstitch entire seam $\frac{1}{8}$ in (3 mm) in from edge. Stitch other side to match.

2. Join underbody from A to B.

3. Stitch the head gusset in the same way, first one side from D to C and then the other side. Continue stitching C to A.

4. Fringe tail end for 1 in (2·5 cm) as in Fig 2a. Then roll lengthwise and hem (Fig 2b).

5. Stitch body from B to E inserting tail where marked and include in stitching. Turn right side out.

6. Shape the longest piece of wire as front legs (Fig 2c). Bind with adhesive tape, taking particular care to cover the ends. Insert in front legs and stuff all round using small pieces of kapok, pushing in firmly with small stick. Bend the wire for back legs in the same way, bind with adhesive tape, insert and stuff.

7. First stuff the head and then the neck very firmly with small pieces. Now stuff from the other end, gradually ladderstitching from E to D.

Fig 2

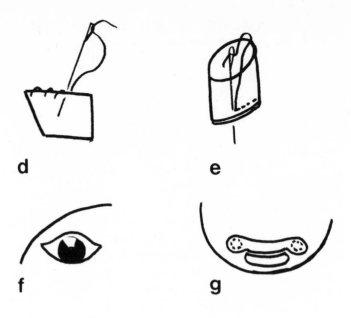

d   e

f   g

Hoofs

First oversew the two straight edges A to B (Fig 2d). Stabstitch the base of hoof to upper, starting at back matching the Bs (Fig 2e). Stuff each hoof and with the seam at the back of leg, hem to base, gradually adding more stuffing as needed.

Horns

Stabstitch together in pairs. Push a small piece of pipe cleaner in each to keep stiff. Stitch one horn on either side of head on seam lines of head gusset $\frac{1}{4}$ in (6 mm) down from top.

Ears

Place ear and lining together right sides facing. Oversew and backstitch as described for body. Turn right side out. Fold in half, A to A, with lining on the inside, and oversew from A to B. Ladderstitch to head in position just under horns.

Eyes

Hem black pupil to pink eye, then hem eye in place with front corner just touching seam lines of head gusset. Embroider white highlight (Fig 2f).

Lips

Fold upper lip in half lengthwise, with wrong sides facing, and oversew ends A to B. Turn right side out and stuff with a little kapok. Oversew seam and stitch to face. Make lower lip in the same way and stitch under upper lip starting $\frac{1}{8}$ in (3 mm) in and making a slight droop (Fig 2g). With one strand of brown embroidery cotton work two nostrils.

CAT & FIDDLE

MATERIALS

Cat

Long-haired fur fabric, white, 13 in × 24 in (33 cm × 61 cm). Felt scraps, pink, green and white.
Cardboard for stiffening paws.
Stranded cotton, brown and red.
Pipe cleaner.
Kapok for filling.
This cat would make a delightful, washable, cuddly toy for a small child by making the following adjustments: use pink cotton material for paws and inner ears, and leave out the cardboard in foot paws. Embroider eyes. Fill with good quality washable filling.

Fiddle and bow

Felt, brown, 5 in × 7 in (12·5 cm × 18 cm).
Buttonhole twist, biscuit colour, 42 ins (106·5 cm).
Pipe cleaner.
1 press stud No 000.
Kapok for filling.

CUT

Body, ears and tail (making sure you reverse the pattern to make the pair) and head gusset in fur fabric.

Mark out one half of underbody and reverse pattern, place along centre line and mark other half. Then when you cut, the whole of the underbody will be in one piece.

Ear linings, two front paws and two back paws and two under eyes in pink felt.

Two outer eyes in green felt and two pupils in white felt.

Two pieces of cardboard slightly smaller than back paws.

Two fiddle pieces, one bridge piece and two extra pieces, one 7 in × ½ in (18 cm × 1·3 cm) and the other 6 in × ½ in (15 cm × 1·3 cm), in brown felt.

MAKING UP

Cat

1. Place one half of body to underbody, right sides together. Oversew from B to C, and backstitch ¼ in (6 mm) in from this seam. Stitch other side to match.
2. Stitch head gusset to head, first one side and then the other. Close seam A to B.
3. Place two tail pieces together right sides facing and stitch. Turn right side out and stuff very firmly.
4. Stitch from C to E on body, inserting the tail just above C. Turn right side out.
5. Stuff very firmly to get a good shape, gradually ladderstitching the opening as you come to it.
6. Place one fur fabric ear (right side) to felt inner ear and stitch as in Step 1 above. Turn right side out. Run a thread along lower edge and draw up. Hem in position on cat, pink side under (Figs 3a and 3b).
7. Place one white pupil in centre of green eye and hem all round. Place eye on pink under eye (Fig 3c) and hem in place, gradually putting in a little stuffing to make a rounded effect. Finally hem the whole eye in place on the head with the inner point meeting the seam of head gusset (Fig 3d). With one strand of cotton, embroider red nose and mouth (Fig 3e).
8. On front paws trim fur fairly short and hem pink felt palm in place.
9. Trim fur on back paws to match, and hem on pink felt paw from G to F both sides. Slip cardboard foot piece in and finish hemming from F to F. With two strands of brown cotton, embroider divisions on paws.
10. Finish neck with a bow.

Fig 3

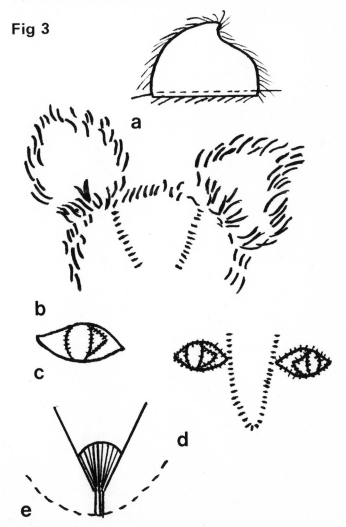

Fiddle

1. Stab stitch 7 in × ½ in (18 cm × 1·3 cm) strip of felt from A to A onto one side of fiddle body (Fig 4a). Stitch on other side to match. Stuff firmly, but keep flat.
2. Cut 1½ in (4 cm) from pipe cleaner and push into open end of fiddle. Gradually stab stitch the thin end pieces together, adding a little stuffing (Fig 4b).
3. Put a small piece of kapok in centre of bridge piece. Fold B to B and stab stitch the three sides. Ladderstitch bridge piece to fiddle, folded edge up.
4. Thread needle with biscuit buttonhole twist, knot the end, and beginning ¾ in (2 cm) from top of fiddle, insert the needle ⅛ in (3 mm) in from edge, take thread over bridge and make a stitch ½ in (1·3 cm) in and ¾ in (2 cm) up from lower edge. Take the thread up again over bridge to top and make another stitch close to first one. Make two more strings in the same way (Fig 4c). Bend top over (Fig 4d).

Fig 4

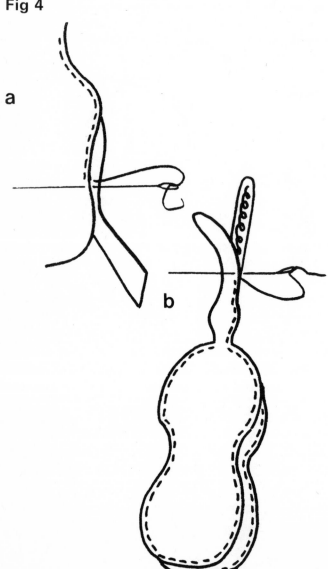

a

b

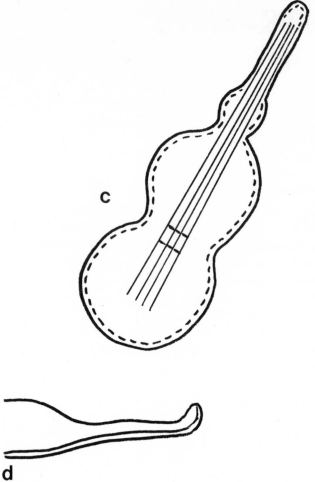

c

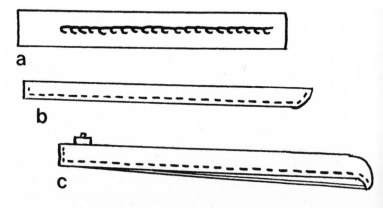

d

Bow

Lay pipe cleaner on brown felt 6 in × ½ in (15 cm × 1·3 cm) as in Fig 5a. Fold over and stabstitch the whole length, rounding off one edge (Fig 5b). Bend rounded top. With biscuit buttonhole twist, make five long strands from rounded top to 1½ in (4 cm) from bottom of bow. Stitch one half of press stud on top (Fig 5c). Stitch the other half of press stud on right inner paw of the cat. The fiddle will fit quite well under the neck and rest on the arm.

Fig 5

a

b

c

LAUGHING DOG

MATERIALS

Long pile nylon fur fabric, grey, 9 in × 29 in (23 cm × 73·5 cm). Original used simulated persian.
Felt, small pieces pink, yellow and black.
Pair of button eyes or black and blue felt.
Wire, 16 gauge, 10 in (25·5 cm) for front legs, and 12 in (30·5 cm) for back legs.
Length of pink stranded cotton for mouth.

CUT

Two bodies, two underbodies, two tails and four ears in fur fabric, making sure you reverse the pattern to make the second of each pair. (Using long pile fur fabric, you can either clip it like a poodle dog's or leave it long all over. Clipping instructions appear at the end of this section.) The nose in black felt, the tongue in pink felt, two eyes in blue felt and two pupils in black felt.

MAKING UP

1. Place one half of underbody to body, right sides facing and oversew the edges from A to B. Backstitch $\frac{1}{4}$ in (6 mm) in from this seam. Stitch other side to match.
2. Stitch from A to B on underbody.
3. Stitch from B to C on body, and from A to D.
4. Turn body right side out.
5. Bend the wire to shape for front legs and back legs (Figs 6a and b). Bind wire with adhesive tape, and place in position as indicated by dotted lines on pattern.
6. Stuff very firmly all round wire, then stuff the head and body, gradually closing with ladderstitch from D to C.
7. Place the ears together in pairs, right sides together, and stitch all round from A to B (Fig 6c), leaving bottom open. Backstitch $\frac{1}{4}$ in (6 mm) in from edge. Turn right side out and ladderstitch to head at dotted line on pattern.
8. Bring one A and C of nose together and oversew on wrong side from A to B. Stitch other side to match. Turn right side out and hem in position on the head, adding a little stuffing as required to give a nice firm tip.
9. With one strand of embroidery cotton, embroider the open mouth, and stitch on the red tongue (Fig 6d).
10. The original has glass eyes, but for a very small child felt is better. To make them, hem the pupil to the eye, adding a little stuffing. Embroider a white highlight with one strand of embroidery thread. Then hem the eye to head in position as shown on pattern.
11. Place the two tail pieces together, right sides facing, and stitch all round except short ends. Turn right side out and stuff firmly. Ladderstitch in position so that the tail is quite straight (Fig 6e).
12. Now have some fun trimming him. Of course, he can be left a rather cuddly, shaggy dog, but the pert little poodle was cut as follows: trim the tail quite close on the straight part, to accentuate the uncut top. Clip $\frac{1}{2}$ in (1·3 cm) all the way along back of body, and trim face under ears and between eyes. Trim the neck leaving sides round mouth and under chin for beard. Leave the top of head long. Trim a band all round body as shown by dotted line on pattern. Trim all round paws.
13. Make a collar with a piece of bright coloured felt $\frac{3}{4}$ in (2 cm) wide to fit neck and overlap $\frac{3}{4}$ in (2 cm). Stick several different coloured circles (a leather punch is a good way to make these) on collar with a little Copydex to form pattern. Cut one end to a point and fasten with a small press stud (Fig 6f).

Fig 6

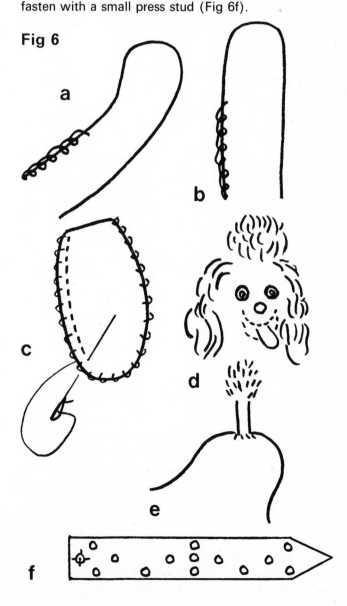

THE DISH

MATERIALS

Felt, flesh-coloured, $10\frac{1}{2}$ in × 7 in (26·7 cm × 18 cm) for dish; brown, 16 in × 7 in (40·6 cm × 18 cm) for legs, arms, dish-edge and head-back, and two pieces $5\frac{1}{4}$ in × 1 in (13·3 cm × 2·5 cm) for shoe uppers; small pieces white, red, bright blue and black for mouth and eyes.

Chamois leather, small piece for soles.

Pipe cleaners.

Thread to match felt.

Kapok for filling.

CUT

All pieces in felt as directed on pattern and in materials described above.

Two soles in chamois leather and two in cardboard.

(Twenty-seven pieces in all including two cardboard soles.)

MAKING UP

1. Start with the eyes. Hem small white highlight on black pupil. Then hem pupil onto blue eye piece, and the blue onto large white eye piece. Make the other eye to match and hem both in place on one of the dish pieces. Hem the mouth in position (Fig 7a).

2. Place dish edge on top of face and tack to keep in position. Hem all round inner edge (Fig 7a). Put aside. Tack head back onto other dish piece and hem inner edge (Fig 7b). Put aside.

3. Stabstitch two arm pieces together all round except short edge between A and B. Cut five lengths of pipe cleaner for each arm. Bend the end of each piece back on itself and pad with a little stuffing. Push five padded ends into felt arm piece and stitch between each to make fingers. Stitch end of arm in position on wrong side of face (Fig 7h).

4. Cut three pieces of pipe cleaner for each leg. Bend to shape and bind with stuffing (Fig 7d). Stitch two pieces of front leg from A to B (Fig 7c). Place pipe cleaners inside the leg and finish stitching all round. Using small running stitches, stitch all round edge of one chamois leather sole (Fig 7e). Do not fasten off. Place a cardboard sole inside and pull stitches over edge. Fasten off by taking long stitches from side to side five or six times (Fig 7e). Take one of the $5\frac{1}{4}$ in × 1 in (13·3 cm × 2·5 cm) brown felt pieces, and starting at centre back, stabstitch to sole (Fig 7f). Stabstitch centre back seam. Stabstitch felt shoe piece to top of shoe, stuffing firmly with kapok as you sew. Cut slit in top of shoe, insert leg and hem in place (Fig 7g). Make back leg in the same way. Stitch legs in place on body (Fig 7h).

5. Stabstitch face of dish to back, stitching through three and four thicknesses where necessary, and stuffing firmly before finishing the final 3 in (7·6 cm).

Fig 7

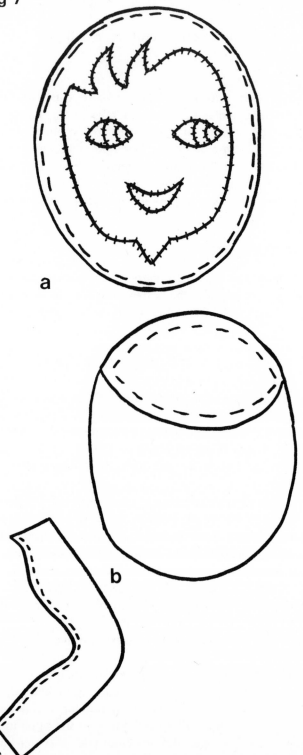

a

b

c

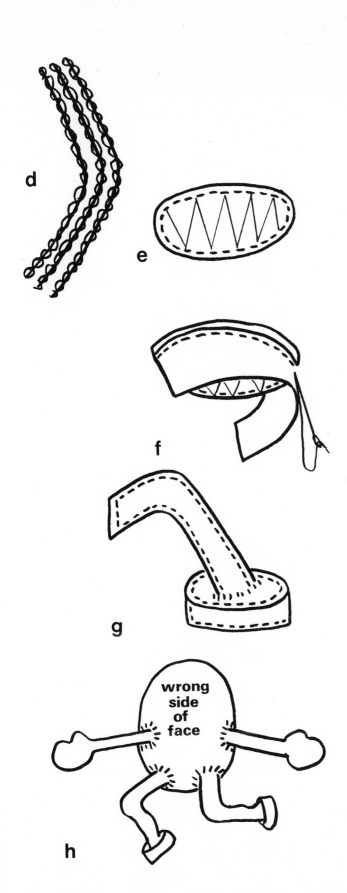

d

e

f

g

wrong
side
of
face

h

SPOON

MATERIALS

Felt, flesh-coloured, 8 in × 11 in (20·3 cm × 28 cm) for spoon and arms; black, 11 in × 2 in (28 cm × 5 cm), and oddments; green, 2 squares 2½ in (6·4 cm) and one circle 4½ in (11·5 cm) in diameter; gold, 3½ in × 5½ in (9 cm × 14 cm) for hair; small pieces of blue and white for eyes and red for mouth.
Piece of wood 10 in (25·4 cm) long, ½ in (1·3 cm) in diameter.
Thread to match felts.
Embroidery cotton, one strand, red.
Kapok for filling.

CUT

All pieces in felt according to pattern (seventeen pieces) and in materials described above.

MAKING UP

1. Begin with the eyes. Hem white highlight on black pupil. Hem pupil on blue eye piece, and then the blue on large white eye piece (Fig 8a). Now hem the whole eye on face. Repeat procedure for the other eye. Hem mouth in position on face. Backstitch the line for open mouth in one strand of red embroidery cotton (Fig 8b).
2. Tack and stitch the front and back hair in position on head pieces.
3. Place the two head pieces together, wrong sides facing, and stabstitch all the way round except neck edge.
4. Wrap the 11 in × 2 in (28 cm × 5 cm) piece of black felt round the wood, and stabstitch along the three sides to close.
5. Stuff the head rather flatly. Push the end of covered stick into head and stuff round the edges until it fits quite firmly. Hem the edge of neck to felt stick.
6. Stabstitch the arm pieces together in pairs, and stuff. Oversew the ends and stitch on each side of stick from A to B, thumbs uppermost (Fig 8c).
7. Trim all the edges of the green felt squares with pinking shears. Place one piece at back of spoon and stitch, ¼ in (6 mm) from edge, to neck (Fig 8d). Place the other piece of green felt to front of neck and stitch in the same way. Stabstitch front and back shoulders together. Press the neck pieces down to form collar and the shoulders up. At the bottom edge of the front, make a pleat on either side and stitch to fit stick. Pleat the back and stitch in the same way. Cut a ½ in (1·3 cm) hole in centre of green felt circle. Trim round lower

edge with pinking shears. Put the stick through the hole and draw skirt up over the blouse and hem the two together. Make a row of stitches $\frac{1}{8}$ in (3 mm) lower, on the skirt, and gather. This will make a waistband and flute the skirt in a rather pretty way (Fig 8e).

Fig 8

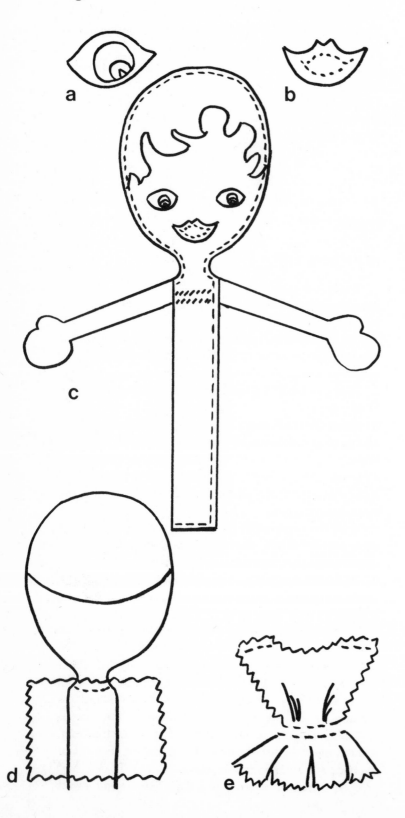

LITTLE BO-PEEP

Little Bo-Peep has lost her sheep
And doesn't know where to find them ;
Leave them alone and they'll come home,
Bringing their tails behind them.

Patterns pp 101–107.

LITTLE BO-PEEP

Height 19 in (48 cm)

MATERIALS

Doll
Felt, flesh-coloured, 15½ in × 12½ in (39·5 cm × 32 cm) for head and arms.
Strong cotton or sateen, 12 in × 11 in (30·5 cm × 28 cm) for body and legs.
Black felt, small pieces for shoes.
White felt, small piece for socks.
Packet of theatrical crêpe hair. This is enough for two dolls.
Embroidery cotton, blue, white, brown, red and black.
Rayon strands for stuffing.
Adhesive tape.
Wooden stick, 4 in (10 cm) long and ¼ in (6 mm) in diameter.
Hair lacquer.

Outfit
White lawn 13 in × 10 in (33 cm × 25·5 cm) for pants.
White lawn 36 in × 13 in (91·5 cm × 33 cm) for petticoat.
Rose coloured sateen 36 in × 12 in (91·5 cm × 30·5 cm) for underskirt.
Green cotton with a small rose pattern 36 in × 12 in (91·5 cm × 30·5 cm) for pannier skirt, and 4 in × 25 in (10 cm × 63 cm) for bodice (this may be substituted with whatever is available).
Small piece of voile or similar for neck and sleeve trimming.
4½ yards (4 metres) of pale green ¼ in (6 mm) wide silk braid, and
1 yard (1 metre) of ⅜ in (1 cm) green ribbon for hat.
16 gauge wire, 16 in (40·5 cm) and
Adhesive tape for crook.
Felt, fawn, 16¾ in × ¾ in (41 cm × 2 cm) and
Narrow green ribbon, ¼ yard (23 cm) for covering and decorating crook.

CUT
Two head-and-arm pieces in flesh-coloured felt.

Two body-and-leg pieces in strong cotton.

Two white sock pieces.

Two black upper-shoe pieces and two black soles.

All outfit pieces according to pattern and using materials described above.

MAKING UP

Body of the doll
Machine- or backstitch the two body-and-leg pieces together, leaving top open for stuffing. Turn right side out and stuff firmly to top of legs. Make two rows of stitching across the top of legs (see pattern) to enable the doll to sit. Finish stuffing body firmly. Turn in a narrow hem at top and oversew. Put aside.

Head
With matching thread, oversew each head dart on the wrong side in the following way : place two outer A's together and oversew to meet inner A. Then place two outer B's together and oversew to meet inner B, and so on, till all darts are sewn. Stitch the other half of head to match. Now place both head-and-arm pieces together, right sides facing, and oversew from A round head to F, then from F round arm to H and A to G. Turn to right side. Stuff the arms halfway. Now make a stabstitch seam across elbow to enable the arm to bend. Continue stuffing to shoulder. Make a stabstitch seam straight down as indicated by dotted line on pattern.

Bind wood with adhesive tape. Now stuff the head firmly, pushing the bound wood in halfway, leaving the other half in neck and chest (Fig 9a). Push small pieces of stuffing all round wood in neck making it very firm. Finish stuffing chest and then hem the chest edge over the top of body edge (Fig 9b).

Shoe and sock
Oversew the sock to shoe upper matching A's. Fold in half at D and oversew from top of sock C to bottom centre of shoe. Oversew the tiny heel seam at D. Now oversew the sole to shoe upper matching heel D's (Fig 9c). Turn to right side and stuff very firmly. Hem the top of sock to the bottom of leg (Fig 9b).

Features
Using one strand of white embroidery cotton, satin stitch the whole shape of the eye. Satin stitch the blue shape on top of the white, and work the black pupil and

white highlight in the same way. Using brown embroidery cotton, backstitch the outline (Fig 9d). Work the eyebrows in brown. Work the mouth in red satin stitch with a black backstitch dividing line (Fig 9e).

Fig 9

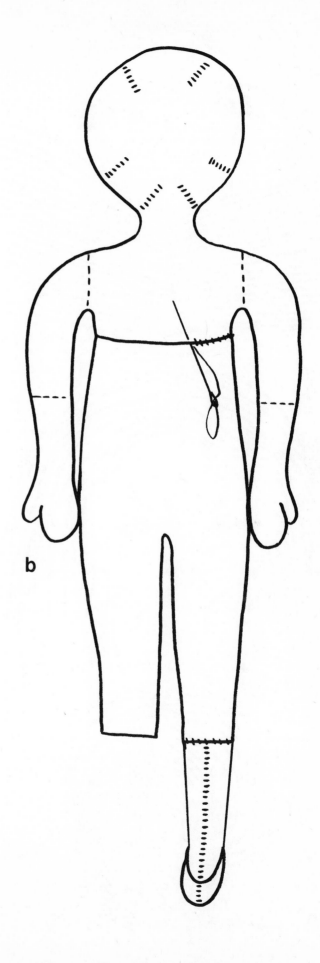

a

b

c

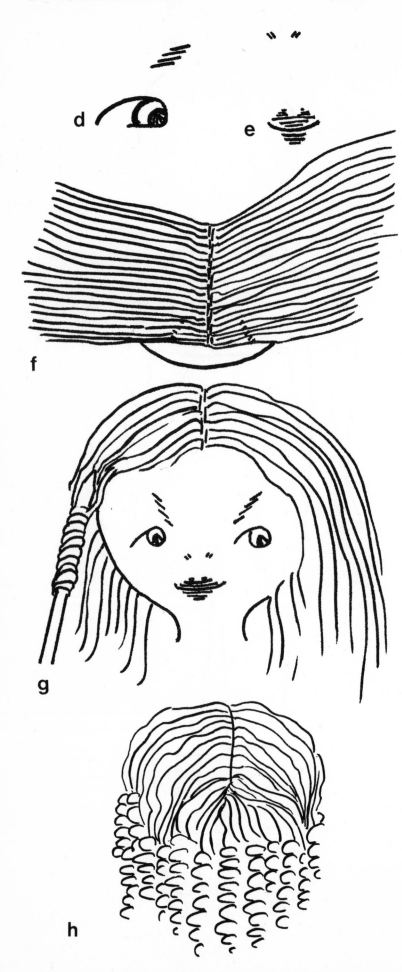

d

e

f

g

h

i

Hair

Bo-Peep's hair is parted in the centre and falls in ringlets at the sides (Fig 9h and i). It is made from crêpe hair which is purchased in a plaited coil, but as one coil is enough for two dolls, you will have to cut it in half. Unplait one half, and place the centre of this on the centre front of doll's head, at the hairline. Gradually ease it out, and backstitch a centre parting with double flesh-coloured thread (Fig 9f). Divide the hair into ten parts. Make each part into a curl by easing the hair sideways so that it covers the head, and, starting at the end, wind each section round a pencil to the required length (Fig 9g). Spray the curl well with lacquer and leave for about an hour.

Pants

Stitch front, back and leg seams. Make a tiny hem on each leg unless it is selvedge, in which case it can be left. Turn to right side and press. Put on doll and hem to the body at waist. Do not turn this edge under or there will be too much bulk at the waistline. Run a gathering thread round leg of pants $\frac{1}{2}$ in (1·3 cm) from bottom. Pull up to fit, and stitch to doll at ankle.

Petticoat

Join the two short sides of the petticoat piece together. Press. Make $\frac{1}{2}$ in (1·3 cm) hem all round lower edge on wrong side. Then make $\frac{1}{2}$ in (1·3 cm) tuck on right side just above hem. Press. Run a thread round top of petticoat. Put it on the doll and pull up to fit. Adjust so that the bottom of the hem comes level with the bottom of the pant frill. Hem petticoat to doll at waist.

Underskirt

Make a pink sateen under-skirt in the same way as petticoat, but do not make a tuck in this.

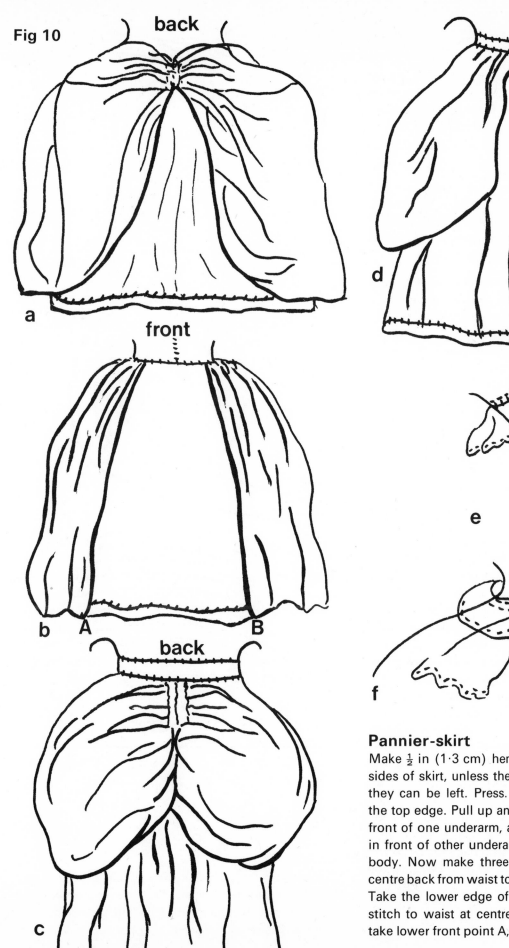

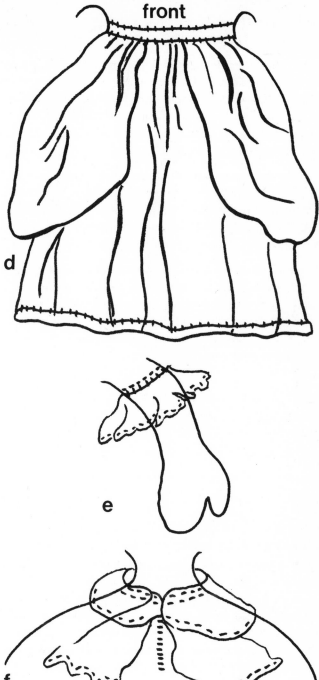

Pannier-skirt

Make ½ in (1·3 cm) hem at lower edge and two short sides of skirt, unless these are selvedge, in which case they can be left. Press. Run a gathering thread along the top edge. Pull up and pin to body, 1 in (2·5 cm) in front of one underarm, around back and 1 in (2·5 cm) in front of other underarm, leaving front clear. Hem to body. Now make three rows of gathering stitches at centre back from waist to hem. Pull up to 2½ in (6·4 cm). Take the lower edge of gathered part, turn under and stitch to waist at centre back (Figs 10a and b). Now take lower front point A, turn under and fasten at centre back waist. Take lower front point B and fasten to match (Figs 10c and d).

Stitch shoulder, sleeve and underarm seams of bodice. Turn to right side. Press. Put on doll. Fold under a small turning around neck edge, right front and lower edge of bodice. Pin to body on top of skirts. Beginning at waist edge of left front F, hem to E, round neck, down right front and round waist.

Roll stitch a very narrow edging round sleeve flounce edge. Cut a small circle in centre, and ease on to doll's arm just below elbow. Stitch to arm. Pull the sleeve over the stitching, make a narrow turning and hem to arm (Fig 10e). Finish other sleeve to match.

Roll stitch a very narrow edging round all sides of neck trimming, fold in half lengthwise and lay round neck. Catch the underpiece to dress with short tacking stitches. Cross the two front pieces and gather in centre. Take several stitches over and over the centre to suggest knot (Fig 10f).

Hat

This is quite attractive and simple to make. The silk braid can sometimes be picked up quite cheaply in a market, and when made up looks like fine straw.

Begin at centre of crown. With matching thread, and using small running stitches, sew along one edge of braid for 3 ins (7·6 cm) as shown in Fig 11a. Pull up to form a circle (Fig 11b). Still using small running stitches, continue sewing the inner edge of braid to the outer edge of circle, easing where necessary, to keep flat (Fig 11c). When the top of crown measures $2\frac{1}{4}$ in (5·7 cm) across, draw the braid fairly tight so that the next circle turns down. Then carry on round and round until the crown is 1 in (2·5 cm) deep. Gradually make the next rounds a little looser so that each one stands a little further away. When ten rounds of the brim have been completed, finish off neatly by turning the end under and hemming to the previous round on the inside. Stitch one end of the ribbon to the left side above the brim, wrap it around the hat and secure. Now just make a small loop, secure it with two small stitches, and twist ribbon so that it comes down over the brim. Take the other end of ribbon and make another loop. Attach to the right side of hat on top of the band. Cut the ribbon in half. Now stand the hat upside down on a clean sheet of paper and spray with hair lacquer. Leave for at least an hour, and then put on doll. Tie under the chin in a bow (Fig 11d).

Fig 11

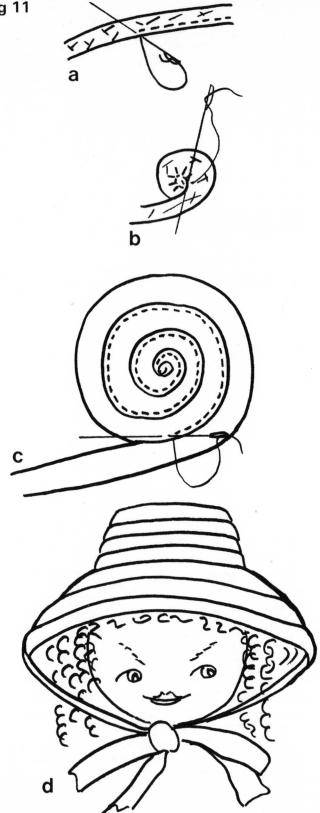

Crook

Cover wire with adhesive tape, taking particular care that the ends are covered. Stab stitch the fawn felt along the length of the crook. Bend the top of crook and finish with a small bow (Fig 11e).

e

SHEEP

MATERIALS

Felt, white, 10 in × 14 in (25·4 cm × 35·6 cm), makes two sheep; black, 5½ in × 2 in (14 cm × 5 cm) for each sheep.
Two pieces 16 gauge wire 6 in (15·2 cm) long.
Adhesive tape.
Short length of black embroidery cotton (single strand).

CUT

All pieces according to pattern and using materials above.

MAKING UP

Sheep No 1

1. Oversew the black face piece to face on body at dotted line. Cut the white piece off close to seam (Figs 12a and b). Stitch the black triangle shaped piece to the front of head gusset matching Ls along dotted line. Cut the white piece off close to seam (Fig 12c).
2. Oversew one piece of underbody to body from A to C, B to D and E to F. Stitch the other half of body and underbody to match. Oversew two pieces of underbody together from A to B.
3. Fold the tail in half lengthwise, matching Bs, and stabstitch from B to M. Cut a slit in the end (Figs 12d and e). Lay tail on right side of body between the two sections at B, stitched side facing down. Stabstitch body from B to G taking needle through tail as well (Fig 12f).
4. Oversew head gusset, using black cotton, from K to L on both sides of face. Using white cotton, oversew from K to H both sides, gently easing gusset into place. Oversew from L to A. Turn and press seams gently with thumbnail.
Cover wire with adhesive tape, taking care to cover ends securely. Using small pieces, stuff the head quite firmly.
5. Bend one piece of covered wire to shape and insert in front legs as indicated by dotted line on pattern.

Push very small pieces of stuffing round wire in the legs. Starting at back of leg hem the black hoof round lower end of leg and close up the front seam. Push a little more stuffing to cover end of wire. Stabstitch the sole of hoof to upper, adding a little stuffing as necessary (Fig 12g). Finish other leg to match. Stuff neck and front to top of leg. Bend other piece of wire to shape for back legs. Insert in back legs and complete as for the front ones. Stuff the hind quarters.
6. Now beginning at front again, complete stuffing, gradually ladderstitching the seam H to G.
7. Place two ear pieces together and oversew, leaving straight edge open. Turn two corners of straight edge to centre and oversew for ¼ in (6 mm) (Fig 12h). Ladderstitch ear to head, seam facing down. Refer to pattern for position.
8. Hem white eye piece to black eye piece. Then hem the whole eye in place on head. Refer to pattern for position. Using a single strand of black embroidery cotton, work the mouth in backstitch (Fig 12i). Hem a small black patch to the lower front of each leg.

Sheep No 2

This sheep has found a nice tasty patch of grass to eat. He is made in exactly the same way as Sheep A.

Fig 12

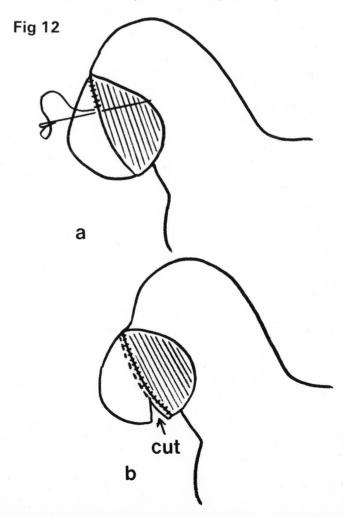

a

cut

b

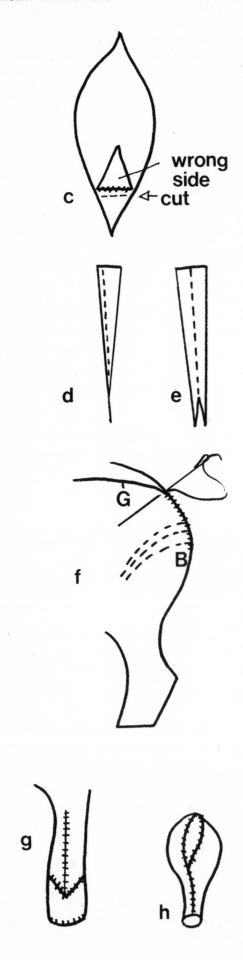

c

wrong
side

← cut

d

e

G

f

B

g

h

i

LITTLE MISS MUFFET

Little Miss Muffet sat on a tuffet
Eating her curds and whey ;
There came a great spider who sat down
  beside her,
And frightened Miss Muffet away.

Fig 13

Patterns pp 101–109.

LITTLE MISS MUFFET

Height 19 in (48 cm).

MATERIALS

Doll

Felt, flesh-coloured, 15½ in × 12½ in (40 cm × 32 cm) for head and arms.

Strong cotton or sateen, 12 in × 11 in (30·5 cm × 28 cm) for body and legs.

Felt, black, small piece for shoes.

Felt, white, small piece for socks.

Ball of pale yellow thick embroidery cotton or silk for hair.

Embroidery cotton, blue, white, brown, red and black.

Rayon strands for stuffing.

Adhesive tape.

Piece of wood, 4 in (10 cm) long, ¼ in (6 mm) in diameter.

Outfit

White embroidery anglaise, 13 in × 10 in (33 cm × 25·4 cm) for pants, and 9 in × 36 in (23 cm × 91·4 cm) for petticoat.

Fine lawn, sprigged with very small navy blue flower, 18 in × 36 in (45·7 cm × 91·4 cm) for dress.

Pale blue ribbon ¼ in × 12 in (6 mm × 30·5 cm) for hair band.

CUT

Doll, shoes, socks and pants as for Bo-Peep.

Skirt 9 in × 36 in (91·4 cm × 23 cm) from flowered lawn, and bodice according to pattern from the remainder.

MAKING UP

Make doll exactly the same as Bo-Peep as far as, and including, shoe and sock.

Features

Embroider features as shown in Fig 13a.

a

b

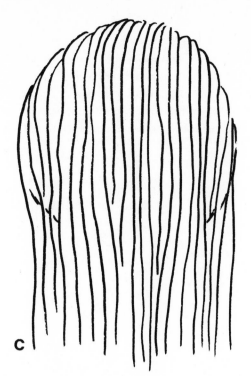

C

Hair

Cut the pale yellow cotton into 18 in (46 cm) lengths and stitch to head in the same way as for Polly Flinders but only on the front half of head. Fold the front hair over the back to fall straight down. Trim. Tie the ribbon round with the bow under the hair at the back. Stitch to keep in place (Fig 13c).

Pants

Cut, make and stitch these to doll in exactly the same way as for Bo-Peep.

Petticoat

Join the two short sides of petticoat piece together. Press. Make a $\frac{3}{4}$ in (2 cm) hem round lower edge on wrong side. Press. Run a thread round top of petticoat. Put on doll and pull thread to fit, arranging gathers evenly all round. Hem the petticoat to doll just under arms.

Dress

Stitch back seams of skirt and make $\frac{1}{2}$ in (1·3 cm) hem round lower edge. Press. Run a gathering thread round top of skirt. Put on doll and draw up to fit, arranging gathers evenly all round. Hem onto petticoat 1 in (2·5 cm) below arms.

Sew darts in front and back bodice pieces. Join shoulder, side and underarm seams. Press and put on doll. Turn under a narrow hem on raw edges of bodice. Starting at back waist, hem back edge to doll from waist to neck, around the neck, and down the other back edge, overlapping $\frac{1}{4}$ in (6 mm) onto the first

edge. Sew around waist overlapping skirt $\frac{1}{4}$ in (6 mm). Turn sleeve ends under and hem to arms. Cut strips of material for frilling 1$\frac{1}{4}$ in (3·2 cm) wide and 1$\frac{1}{2}$ times the length of the hem, neck and cuffs. Join the short seam, press and make a very narrow hem both sides of frill. Run a gathering thread along the centre. Draw up to fit and stitch in place on top of gathering stitches. The skirt frill should be stitched on top of the hem seam. The sleeve frills should be stitched on the extreme edge of sleeve. The neck frill should be stitched to allow one half to stand up prettily round the neck and the other half to lie on top of the dress (Fig 13b).

SPIDER

MATERIALS

Felt, brown, one piece 3 in × 4 in (7·6 cm × 10 cm), four pieces 8$\frac{1}{2}$ in × $\frac{1}{2}$ in (21·6 cm × 1·3 cm), two pieces 2 in × $\frac{1}{2}$ in (5 cm × 1·3 cm), pink, 4 in × 3 in (10 cm × 7·6 cm), scraps of white and black.

Fur fabric, brown, one piece 3 in × 4 in (7·6 cm × 10 cm).
Embroidery thread, black and white.
Wire, four pieces 10 in (25·4 cm) long.
Round black elastic, 8 in (20·3 cm).
Adhesive tape.
Stuffing.

CUT

One body piece from fur fabric according to pattern, and one from brown felt.

Eight boots in pink felt.

Eye parts as indicated on pattern.

MAKING UP

Turn over the end of each wire and bend in position for legs as in Fig 14a. Bind each wire with adhesive tape. Starting at one "foot', fold a length of brown felt round leg and stabstitch seam, finishing at other foot (Fig 14b). Make three more pairs of legs in the same way. Place the felt body piece on top of the fur fabric body piece, right side inside, and oversew round head from A to C, then from B to E and D to F. Backstitch $\frac{1}{4}$ in (6 mm) in from this stitching. Turn to right side. Push one leg of each pair through openings from B to E and D to F. Arrange them to spread on either side of body. Stuff the head firmly, and gradually stuff the body, taking great care to cover top and bottom of legs well. Ladderstitch the opening and sew the leg openings firmly to legs.

Eyes

Hem the black circle on the centre of the pink, and the pink on the centre of the white. Consulting Fig 14f for position, hem eyes to head, adding a little stuffing to make them protrude. With one strand of white embroidery thread, embroider a small highlight in each eye. Embroider the mouth with one strand of black (Fig 14f).

Fig 14

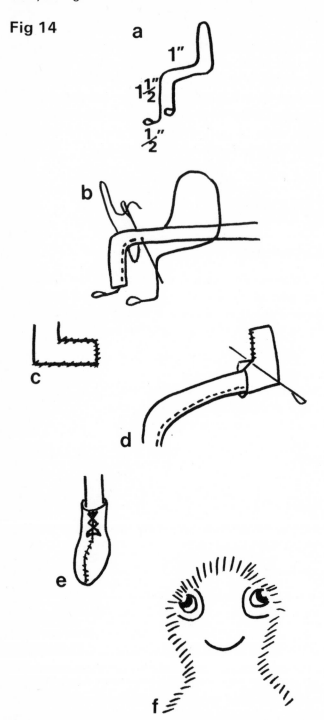

Boots

Fold the boot in half, matching As. Oversew from B to A to C. Turn right side out. Put a small piece of stuffing in toe and put boot on foot. Stabstitch seam from ankle to top of boot. Using one strand of black embroidery thread make two or three cross stitches down the front, finishing with a straight stitch at the bottom, to form laces (Figs 14c, d and e).

LITTLE POLLY FLINDERS

Little Polly Flinders sat among the cinders,
Warming her pretty little toes;
Her mother came and caught her, and whipped her little daughter
For spoiling her nice new clothes.

Patterns pp 101–108.

LITTLE POLLY FLINDERS

Height 19 in (48·3 cm).

MATERIALS

Doll

Felt, flesh-coloured, 15½ in × 12½ in (39·4 cm × 31·8 cm) for head and arms.
Two pieces 5¾ in × 3¼ in (14·6 cm × 8·3 cm) for feet and ankles.
Strong cotton or sateen, 12 in × 11 in (30·5 cm × 28 cm) for body and legs.
Small ball 3-ply auburn wool for hair.
Embroidery cotton, blue, white, brown, red and black.
Rayon strands for stuffing.
Adhesive tape.
Hair lacquer.
Piece of wood, 4 in (10·2 cm) long, ¼ in (6 mm) in diameter.

Outfit

The original dress and pants were made from ½ yard of 36 in (45·7 cm × 91·4 cm) cotton print, with small mauve flowers on white background.
1¾ yards (160 cm) narrow embroidered ribbon or braid.
1¼ yards (114·3 cm) of 1 in (2·5 cm) green ribbon.

CUT

Doll exactly the same as Bo-Peep as far as, but not including, shoe and sock.

Two ankle-and-foot pieces and two front-of-foot pieces from pattern in flesh-coloured felt.

Pants, back and front bodice and sleeves according to pattern, and a piece 7½ in × 36 in (19 cm × 91·4 cm) for skirt.

MAKING UP

Make doll exactly the same as Bo-Peep as far as shoe and sock.

Ankle and foot

Fold As together and oversew from A to B on ankle-and-foot piece. Oversew front piece from C to E and F to D. Now oversew round toes from E to D. Turn to right side and push in a little stuffing. Stabstitch between toes (Fig 15a). Finish stuffing firmly and hem to bottom of leg, making sure the big toe is on the inside. Make another foot in the same way, but reverse the front panel so that the big toe comes on the inside.

Fig 15

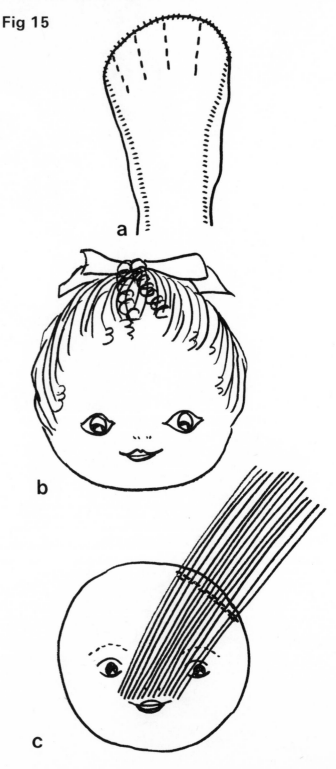

a

b

c

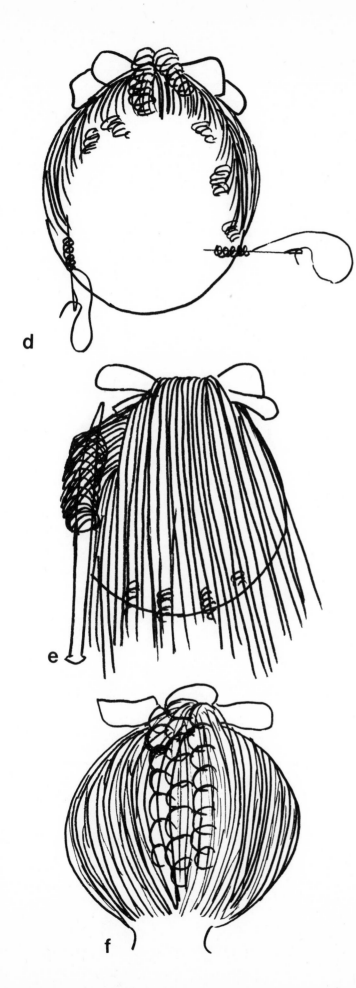

d

e

f

Features
Embroider as shown in Fig 15b.

Hair
Cut the wool in 18 in (46 cm) lengths. Lay this all round the head with the centre of wool to hair line (Fig 15c). Draw all the hair to the top of head and bind tightly with a little wool. This will look like a pony tail. To make the wispy curls around the hairline, take one strand of wool threaded in a slim darning needle, secure the wool to the head and bring out the needle where the curl is to begin. Wind the wool five times round the needle. Take a small stitch where the curl is to end and take the needle back through the curl rings to beginning (Fig 15d).

Divide the pony tail into eight parts for loose curls at the back and two short lengths to make two small curls to fall over front. To make these curls, spray one part with lacquer and, starting at the end, wind wool round a pencil or wood of similar dimensions. Spray the finished curl and leave until dry before removing pencil — at least an hour (Fig 15e and f).

Cut 18 in (46 cm) of ribbon and tie in a bow round the top of the pony tail.

Pants
Make in the same way as for Little Bo-Peep, but before stitching to body, sew embroidery to the bottom of legs and leave to hang loose.

Dress
Stitch seam at back of skirt and make $\frac{1}{2}$ in (1·3 cm) hem at the bottom. Stitch embroidery round lower edge of hem. Gather top of skirt and stitch to doll just under arms, keeping all fullness to the back. Join shoulder and underarm seams of bodice. Join sleeve seams. Gather tops of sleeves and stitch into armholes. Press and put on doll. Turn under a small hem round neck edge, down back and round lower edge of bodice. Pin lower edge to body on top of skirt. Hem the bodice to the doll beginning at waist edge of right back, up to neck line, round neck, down left back and round waist. Gather lower edge of sleeves and hem to arm forming a puff. Stitch a piece of embroidery round bottom of sleeve and round neck (Fig 16). Wrap the ribbon round waist and hem top and bottom, with the lower edge coming just below the seam on dress. Make a small tuck in ribbon under the arms, and finish with a bow at the centre back.

Fig 16

a

POLLY PUT THE KETTLE ON

**Polly, put the kettle on,
Polly, put the kettle on,
Polly, put the kettle on,
We'll all have tea.**

Patterns pp 101–111.

POLLY

Height 19 in (48 cm).

MATERIALS

Doll

Felt, flesh-coloured, 15½ in × 12½ in (39·4 cm × 32 cm) for head and arms.
Strong cotton or sateen, 12 in × 11 in (30·5 cm × 28 cm) for body and legs.
Felt, black, small piece for shoes.
Felt, white, small piece for socks.
Ball of black 3-ply wool for hair.
Embroidery cotton, black, white and brown.
Rayon strands for stuffing.
Adhesive tape.
Piece of wood 4 in (10·2 cm) long, ¼ in (6 mm) in diameter.

Outfit

White lawn, 13 in × 10 in (33 cm × 25·4 cm) for pants.
White lawn, 36 in × 13 in (91·4 cm × 33 cm) for petticoat.
Lawn with small sprigged design, 36 in × 18 in (91·4 cm × 46 cm) for dress.
Fancy organdie or stiff voile, 8 in × 6 in (20·3 cm × 15·2 cm), and 2 in × 30 in (5 cm × 76·2 cm) for apron and 8 in (20·3 cm) square for cap.
Lace, 2 in (5 cm) wide; 11 in (28 cm) for collar, and 10 in (25·4 cm) for cuffs.
Felt, copper-brown, 9 in × 7 in (23 cm × 18 cm).
Small piece of cardboard.
Piece of thin cord or string for kettle.

CUT

Doll and pants exactly the same as Bo-Peep, including shoe and sock.

Bodice pieces in sprigged lawn according to pattern, and another piece 36 in × 11 in (91·4 cm × 28 cm) for skirt.

Mob cap according to pattern.

Two upper kettle pieces, two lower kettle pieces, two spouts, one base, one lid and one knob in copper-brown felt.

One handle, 7 in × ½ in (18 cm × 1·3 cm) in copper-brown felt.

One base in cardboard.

MAKING UP

Make doll exactly the same as Bo-Peep including shoe and sock.

Fig 17

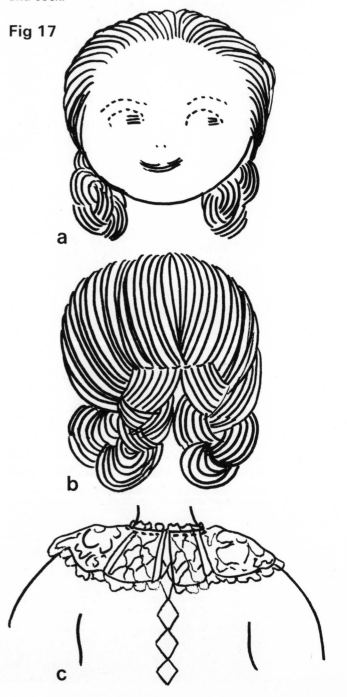

a

b

c

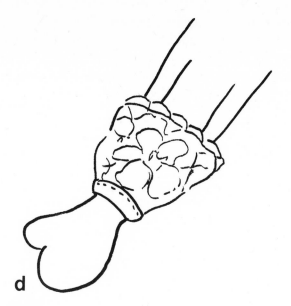

d

Features

Consulting Fig 17a, work the eyes in white, brown and black embroidery cotton (one strand). Work nose and mouth in red.

Hair

Polly's black hair is cut in 20 in (51 cm) lengths, has a centre parting, and each side is made into a plait. Lay the hair across the top of the head and backstitch a centre parting with double flesh-colour thread. Draw hair to back and make into two plaits. Bind each plait at the end with black wool to keep firm. Wind plait forward, tuck ends in and lightly stitch at back (Fig 17b).

Pants

Make and stitch these to doll in exactly the same way as for Bo-Peep.

Petticoat

Join the two short sides of petticoat piece together. Press. Make a $\frac{3}{4}$ in (2 cm) hem round lower edge and press. Make a $\frac{1}{2}$ in (1·3 cm) tuck just above hem, and another tuck, $\frac{1}{4}$ in (6 mm), just above that. Press. Run a thread round the top of petticoat. Put on doll and draw up to fit, arranging gathers evenly, and adjust length to leave $\frac{1}{2}$ in (1·3 cm) of the legs of pants showing below. Hem top of petticoat to doll just under arms.

Dress

Stitch back seam of skirt and make a $\frac{3}{4}$ in (2 cm) hem at lower edge. Press. Run a gathering thread around the top, put it on the doll and draw up to fit, arranging gathers evenly all round. Hem to doll at waist. Stitch shoulder, sleeve and underarm seams of bodice. Turn to right side, press and put on doll. Make a small hem round neck edge, right fronts and lower edge of bodice. Pin to body on top of skirt. Beginning at waist edge of left front A, hem to B, round neck, down right front and around waist. Turn sleeve edge under and hem to wrist. Embroider six diamond-shaped buttons from neck edge to waist (Fig 17c).

Collar

Run a thread along the edge of the collar lace and draw up to fit neck. Stitch to neckline of dress, starting at centre front and arranging gathers evenly (Fig 17c).

Cuffs

Cut the cuff lace in half. Join the edges of one half together and run a thread around the edge. Put it over the sleeve, pull up to fit, and hem to wrist. Stitch to arm again $\frac{1}{4}$ in (6 mm) above the wrist edge (Fig 17d).

Apron

Make $\frac{1}{4}$ in (6 mm) hem on both 6 in (15·2 cm) edges and one 8 in (20·3 cm) edge. Gather the other edge to $3\frac{1}{2}$ in (9 cm) and arrange gathers evenly. Fold the 2 in (5 cm) band in half lengthwise, and sew the apron into the fold. Hem the edges of the tie ends. Press and tie on doll.

Mob cap

Make a narrow hem all around the edge. Run a gathering thread above this hem, $1\frac{1}{2}$ in (4 cm) from edge. Put it on the doll and draw up to fit (Fig 18a).

KETTLE

Stitch darts in both halves of lower kettle. With wrong sides facing, oversew halves together, and then to felt base. Place cardboard base in position and stuff kettle firmly (Fig 18b). Put aside. Stitch darts in both halves of upper kettle. Oversew halves together and turn to right side. Stuff firmly. On right side, stabstitch upper and lower kettle pieces together (Fig 18c). Run a gathering thread around the lid $\frac{1}{8}$ in (3 mm) in from edge. Draw up. Put in a little stuffing, and hem to top of kettle. Make the knob in the same way, and hem to centre of lid (Fig 18d). Oversew spout from A to B and B to C. Turn to right side and stuff firmly. Hem in place on kettle (Fig 18e). Place a piece of thin cord or string lengthwise along centre of handle, fold the felt

Fig 18

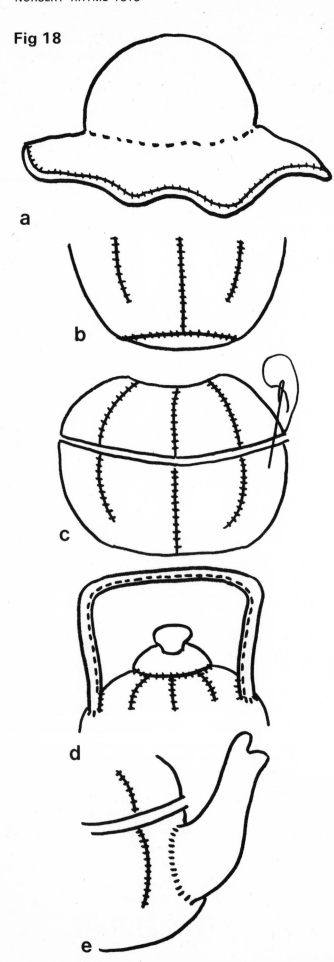

a

b

c

d

e

over it and stabstitch the edges together. Open one end and hem to side of kettle, stitched side facing downwards. Finish other side to match. Bend handle to shape, and make a few stitches at each corner to hold. Stitch to the centre of doll's right hand.

LITTLE JACK HORNER

Little Jack Horner sat in a corner
Eating his Christmas pie ;
He put in his thumb and pulled out a
**   plum**
And said "What a good boy am I!"

Patterns pp 112–116.

LITTLE JACK HORNER

Height 16½ in (42 cm).

MATERIALS

Doll

Felt, flesh-coloured, 16 in × 11½ in (40·6 cm × 29·2 cm) for head and arms.
Strong cotton or sateen, 10 in × 11½ in (25·4 cm × 29·2 cm) for body and legs.
Embroidery thread, white, blue and black.
Fur fabric, long pile, 6 in × 6½ in (15·2 × 16·5 cm) for hair.
Wooden stick, 5 in × ½ in diameter (12·7 cm × 1·3 cm diameter).
Adhesive tape.

Outfit

Green velvet, 14 in × 8¾ in (35·6 cm × 22·2 cm) for trousers.
White lawn, 18 in × 13 in (45·7 cm × 33 cm) for blouse.
Felt, black, 6¼ in × 3¼ in (16 cm × 8·3 cm) for shoes.
Felt, white, 6¼ in × 10½ in (16 cm × 26·7 cm) for socks, pie dish and buttons.
Felt, gold, 5¼ in × 3½ in (13·3 cm × 9 cm) for buckles and pie crust.
Felt, plum-coloured, 2¾ in × 1½ in (7 cm × 3·8 cm) for plum and pie portion.
Chamois leather, 2½ in × 3 in (6·4 cm × 7·6 cm) for shoe soles.
Small piece of cardboard for soles.

CUT

All pieces in materials described above, as follows :

Two head-and-arm pieces, two body-and-leg pieces, two socks, two shoe fronts and two shoe uppers, four chamois leather soles, two cardboard soles, two gold buckles and one hair piece.

Two trouser pieces, one blouse back (placing dotted line to fold of fabric) two blouse fronts, two collar

pieces and one piece 5 in × 1½ in (12·7 cm × 3·8 cm) for front frill.

Four buttons, one pie dish base, two pie dish sides, one pie crust, two plum pieces and one pie portion.

MAKING UP

Make doll exactly the same as Bo-Peep as far as, but not including, shoe and sock, which are left until the blouse and trousers have been fitted.

Fig 19

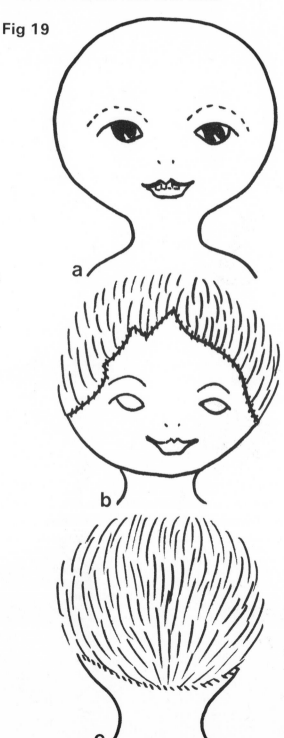

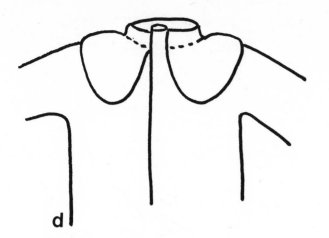

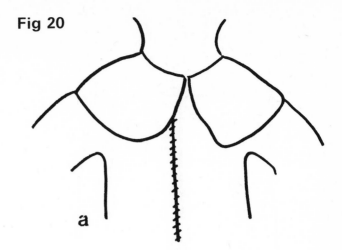

Fig 20

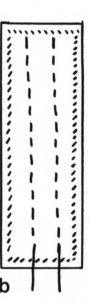

Features

(Fig 19a)

Using one strand of white embroidery cotton, satin stitch the whole of the eye. Satin stitch the blue shape on top of this, then the black shape and finally a small white highlight. Outline the eye with black embroidery thread. Embroider the eyebrows in black and make two small stitches to suggest a nose. The open mouth is worked in red satin stitch. Embroider the top row of teeth in white, and outline just the top of the lower teeth.

Hair

Place the front point of hair A to the centre of the doll's forehead. Turn under a narrow hem all round and stitch to head, easing fullness to the back (Figs 19b and c).

Blouse

Join the shoulder, side and sleeve seams. Make a narrow hem at each cuff and turn blouse to right side. Press. Place the two collar pieces together and stitch all round outer edges. Turn to right side and press. Make a narrow hem along left front edge of blouse. Place the collar round the neck of blouse and stitch evenly all round except for the narrow turning down centre front (Fig 19d). Put the blouse on the doll and hem the left front to the body. Turn the neck edge under and hem to doll's neck (Fig 20a). Hem the two long sides and top edge of frill. Run two threads $\frac{1}{4}$ in (6 mm) apart down centre of frill (Fig 20b). Draw up to fit the front of blouse and attach with seven french knot buttons, starting at the top and working downwards with even spaces (Fig 20c).

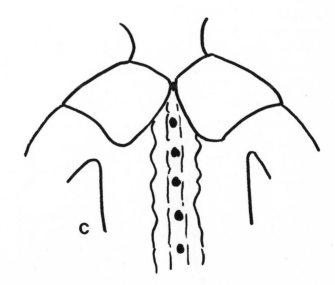

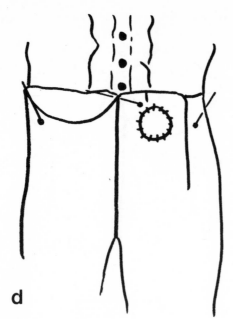

d

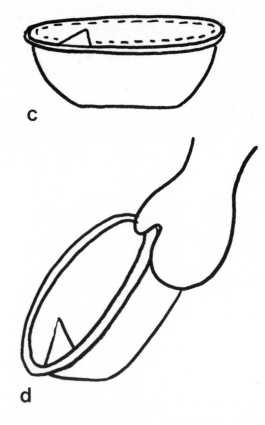

c

d

Trousers

Stitch the two trouser pieces together, wrong sides facing, from A to B and D to B. Then stitch the legs from B to C. Press the seams. Put them on the doll and pin the sides to sides of doll. Pin centre front and back and make a flat pleat to take in extra material on both sides of the two joins (Fig 20d). Make a narrow turning and hem top of trousers to waist of doll. Hem four white felt buttons on the four pleats.

Shoes and socks

Oversew the sock to shoe upper, matching As. Fold in half at D and oversew from C to F. Oversew tiny heel seam E. Put on one side. Oversew the two chamois leather sole pieces together from E to G each side. Turn to right side. Slip the cardboard sole between and ladderstitch opening. On wrong side, oversew the upper to sole matching Es and Fs. Turn to right side and stuff firmly to within $\frac{1}{2}$ in (1·3 cm) of top. Pull over leg and hem. Finish other leg to match. Turn under leg of trousers and catch hem with a few small stitches to hold in place. Hem the shoe front to front of shoe (Fig 21a). Hem the gold buckle to front of shoe (Fig 21b). Finish other shoe to match.

Plum

Oversew two plum pieces together from A to B to A. Turn to right side and stuff. Hem one end of plum between thumb and finger of left hand. Stitch the other end of plum just under lower lip.

Pie

Oversew the ends of two pie dish pieces together. Oversew the base of dish to sides. Turn right side out and stuff to within $\frac{1}{2}$ in (1·3 cm) of top of dish. Stitch the pie portion to pie crust. Place the crust on top of dish and stabstitch the two together $\frac{1}{2}$ in (1·3 cm) in from edge round the top (Fig 21c). Stitch the dish between the thumb and finger of right hand (Fig 21d).

Fig 21

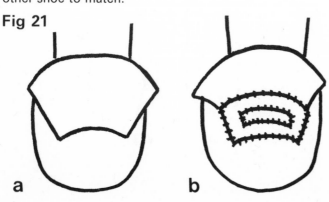

a   b

RIDE A COCK HORSE

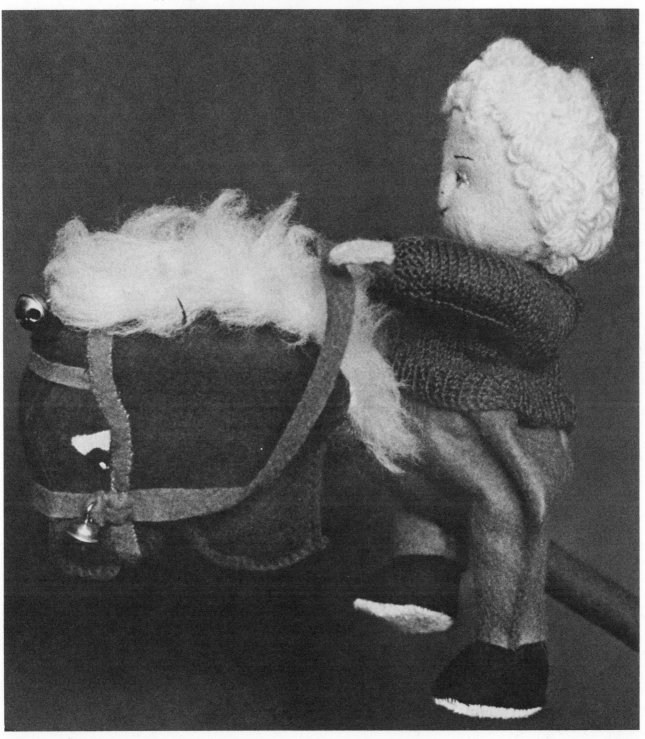

**Ride a cock horse to Banbury Cross
To see a fine lady upon a white horse.
With rings on her fingers and bells on
  her toes,
She shall have music wherever she goes.**

Patterns pp 118–119.

RIDE·A·COCK·HORSE

Height 8 ins (20·3 cm).

MATERIALS

Felt, flesh-coloured, 12 in × 7 in (30·5 cm × 17·8 cm) for the boy; dark brown, 4 in × 8 in (10·2 cm × 20·3 cm) for the horse; fawn, 4 in × 5 in (10·2 cm × 12·7 cm) for jodhpurs; scraps of black for shoes and pupils and white for eyes.
Small piece of chamois leather for shoe soles.
Strip of white long-haired fur fabric.
Small ball yellow 2-ply wool for hair.
Embroidery cotton, blue, white, red, brown and black.
Dowelling, 12 in × $\frac{1}{2}$ in (30·5 cm × 1·3 cm).
Small ball 2-ply emerald wool.
Knitting needles, size 13.
Five press studs, size 000.
Strip of dark brown felt 14 in × 1 in (35·6 cm × 2·5 cm) for horse head gusset.
Three small bells.
Muslin, 2 in (5 cm) square.
Small piece of cardboard.
Three cherry sticks.
Adhesive tape.
Stuffing.
While this toy is based on the nursery rhyme Ride a Cock Horse, the horse part would make a very nice rattle, and the boy doll a mascot. In this case, both the boy's legs should be made from the straight leg pattern.

CUT

All pieces as shown on pattern.

MAKING UP BOY

Starting with the head piece and matching thread, fold two As together and oversew. In the same manner, oversew B to A, C to C and D to D. Work other side to match. This forms the top of the head. Now line the wrong side with stuffing $\frac{1}{2}$ in (1·3 cm) thick and on this place the muslin. This gives a padding on which to

work the features and by so doing, a modelling effect can be obtained. On the right side of work, carefully mark with a light lead pencil the position for the eyes and mouth, remembering to keep them low in the head for a childlike effect. Now embroider the whole eye area with one strand of white embroidery cotton, gently sinking the area and thus raising the centre between the eyes to form a nose. When both eye sockets are covered with white, embroider blue part on top of this, and black pupil on top of the blue. Model the mouth in red, and make two dots for nose. Embroider the brows in backstitch with one strand of brown (Fig 22a). Now oversew the two Es together, and the two Fs. Work other side to match. Oversew from A to G. Turn to right side and fill quite firmly with stuffing (Fig 22b). Put on one side.

Fig 22

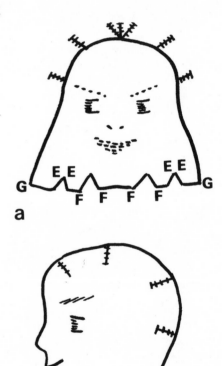

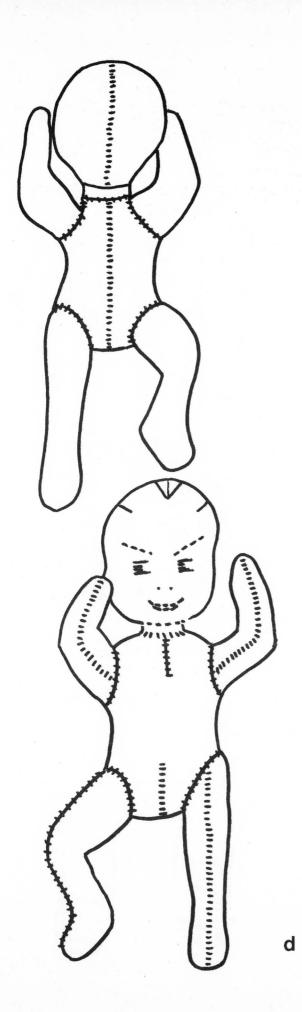

d

Body

Oversew A to A and B to B. Oversew from C to D to A. Turn to right side and stuff very firmly. Run a thread through the top and draw up, but do not finish off for the moment.

Bind three cocktail sticks together with adhesive tape (Fig 22c). Push one end into the body, draw thread up tight and fasten off. Push other end of sticks into head. Ladderstitch head to body, making sure the front of head is over the front of body. Make a neck by back-stitching a row of stitches $\frac{1}{8}$ in (3 mm) up from seam.

Legs

Oversew on wrong side from A to B, to C, to D. Turn to right side and stuff firmly. Hem in position on body (Fig 22d).

Arms

Oversew on wrong side from A to B and from C to D. Run a thread round edge of lower arm, pull up tight and fasten off. Turn and stuff firmly. Stitch arms in place on body (Fig 22d).

Hands

Stabstitch two hand pieces together round fingers from A to B. Stitch lines indicating fingers (Fig 22e). Open wrist end. Insert small piece of stuffing to form palm. Put over end of arm and hem all round.

Shoes

Oversew two pieces of chamois leather together from A to C and from B to C. Turn. Slip piece of cardboard between. Turn ends in and ladderstitch neatly. Starting at C, oversew shoe upper to sole on seamline (Fig 22f). Turn. Pad with a little stuffing. Put on doll. Stitch D across from outside of foot to instep and down to C. Then stitch other side across from instep out. Hem top of shoe to leg (Fig 23a). Make other shoe to match.

Hair

Thread a long darning needle with a long length of yellow wool. Join to crown of head. Lay a fairly thick knitting needle (No 6 or 7) on stitch and wind wool close to head six times round needle. Pass the darning needle through the loops, take a stitch through head under the loops, and bring needle up beside them. Repeat this procedure gradually, working from crown, until the whole head is covered with curls. When working round the face, do not make the placing too regular, but deliberately let a few fall out of place. This will help to give the doll quite a cheeky appearance (Figs 23b and c).

Jodhpurs

Oversew front seam, back seam and inner leg seams from B to C. Put on the doll and stabstitch the side seams on outside. Make a small pleat each side of front and back seams, and also at sides. Stabstitch each pleat in place for ½ in (1·3 cm). Hem the top of jodhpurs to waist of doll (Fig. 23d).

Jersey

(K = Knit; P = Purl; St-St = Stocking-Stitch.)

Using size 13 needles and emerald wool, cast on 30 stitches.

K1 P1 rib for 6 rows. St-St for 10 rows.
Row 17: Increase 20 sts at beginning of row and K to end.
Row 18: Increase 20 sts at beginning of row. K4. P to last 4 sts. K 4.
Next row: K.
Next row: K4. Purl to last 4 sts. K4.
Repeat last two rows 10 times.
Next row: K28. Cast off 14. K28.
Next row: K4. P24.
Next row: K.
Repeat last two rows once.
Next row: K4. P24. Increase 9 sts at end of row.
Next row: K.
Next row: K4. P31. K2.
Repeat these two rows 10 times.
Next row: K.
Next row: Cast off 20. P to last 2 sts. K2.
Next row: K.
Next row: P to last 2 sts. K2.
Repeat last two rows 8 times.
K1 P1 rib for 6 rows.
Cast off.

Fasten wool to neck edge and work to match right side. Press the work on the wrong side with a hot iron over a damp cloth. With right side facing, pick up and knit 36 stitches all round neck edge. K1 P1 rib for 5 rows. Cast off in rib. Stitch side and sleeve seams. Sew press studs on centre back, equal distances apart.

Fig 23

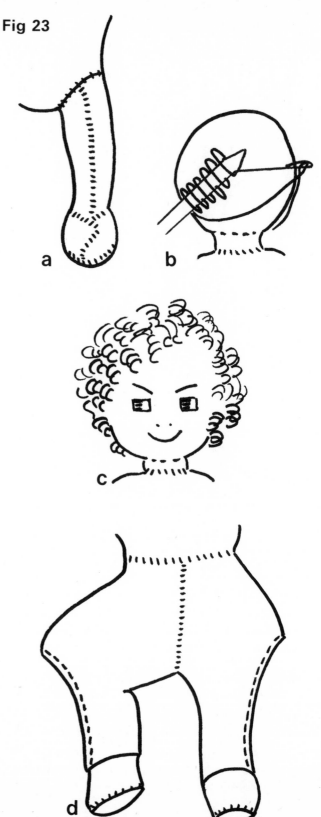

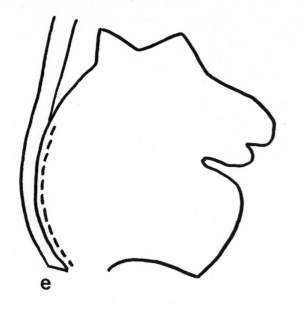

e

Stitch pupil to white eye and embroider white high-light. Hem eyes to head, consulting pattern for position. Embroider nostrils in white. Cut $\frac{1}{4}$ in (6 mm) strips of fawn felt. Place short piece over head in front of ears and stitch ends to head. Place another piece over end of nose and under chin. Stitch in position at mouth edges. Starting at one side of mouth, stitch another piece all the way round, inside mouth, over top of head and down other side to meet the other end. Hem neatly along both sides. Cut a strip of fawn felt for reins. On each end, slip a small bell, turn end of felt back and stitch to each side of mouth. Slip a small bell on a piece of fawn felt 1 in × $\frac{1}{4}$ in (2·5 cm × 6 mm), fold in half and stitch to the centre of head, letting bell just fall over front of forehead (Fig 23f).

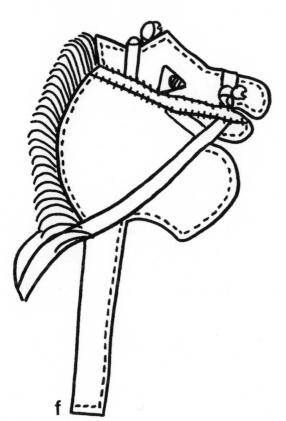

f

MAKING UP HORSE

Take one side of head and stabstitch strip of brown felt all round, starting at lower back edge A, and finishing B (Fig 23e). Stitch the other side of head to other side of strip. Stuff the head, keeping it flat. Cut a strip of dark brown felt to cover stick. Stabstitch this to stick along lower edge and long side. Push the stick into the stuffing in the horse's head. Stitch opening firmly round stick. Turn in edges of fur strip and hem to head from C to A.

LITTLE BOY BLUE

Little Boy Blue, come blow your horn,
The sheep's in the meadow, the cow's
   in the corn.
But where is the boy who looks after
   the sheep?
He's under the haystack, fast asleep.

Patterns pp 117–119.

LITTLE BOY BLUE

Height 9 in (22·8 cm).

MATERIALS

Felt, flesh-coloured, 12 in × 7 in (30·5 cm × 17·8 cm);
small piece of blue for shoe uppers and horn.
Small piece of chamois leather.
Embroidery cotton, blue, white, red, brown and black.
Small ball light brown 3-ply wool for hair.
Three cherry sticks.
Adhesive tape.
Stuffing.
Muslin, 2 in (5 cm) square.
Six long strands of natural raffia for hat.
Blue denim, 6½ in × 13½ in (16·5 cm × 34·3 cm) for
dungarees.
Small ball pale blue 2-ply wool for jersey.
Pair of knitting needles, size 13.
Cardboard for horn.
Five press studs size 000.

CUTTING AND MAKING UP

Cut out and make doll exactly as for Ride-a-Cock-
Horse as far as (and including) shoes, but make two
straight legs and blue upper shoes.
Also cut two horn pieces from blue felt, two from
cardboard, and all dungaree pieces from blue denim.

Fig 24

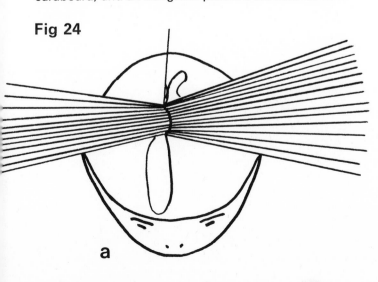

a

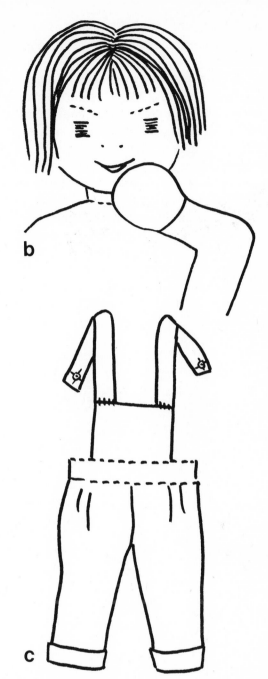

b

c

Hair

Take a large bundle of light brown wool (60 strands)
6 in (15·2 cm) long. Lay across top of head. With
flesh-coloured thread, stitch the centre of the bundle
to the centre of the head (Fig 24a). Stitch another
bundle exactly the same just in front of the last. Fasten
off very securely. Pull the wool down so that it falls
round the head. Cut level with the bottom of the head
all round. Stitch the underlayer of hair at intervals round
head to keep in place. Cut front and taper sides towards
back (Fig 24b).

Jersey

Using pale blue wool, make this in the same way as
for Ride-a-Cock-Horse's.

Dungarees

Join front seams together from A to B. Join back seam from C to D. Stitch leg seams. Make a narrow hem on back opening. Turn in $\frac{1}{8}$ in (3 mm) all round one piece of waistband and tack to top of the dungarees letting it overlap $\frac{1}{8}$ in (3 mm) one side and $\frac{1}{4}$ in (6 mm) the other side at back, and making a pleat each side of front seam to take in the fullness. Turn in $\frac{1}{8}$ in (3 mm) each long side of bib. Fold in half. Stab- or machine-stitch side seams. Tack to centre of waistband. Turn in and tack second waist band piece to the back of the first, and stitch. Fold straps in half right side inside, A to A and B to B. Stitch one short end and long side. Turn and press. Turn in ends and oversew to top of bib front (Fig 24c). Stitch press studs to fasten back opening and one on each end of straps. Try on doll and make a hem on the cuff of each leg. Arrange hem to form a turn-up.

Fig 25

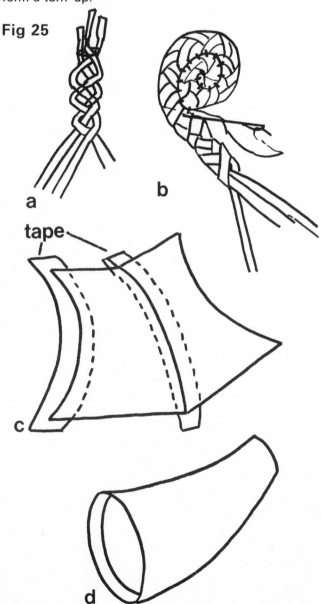

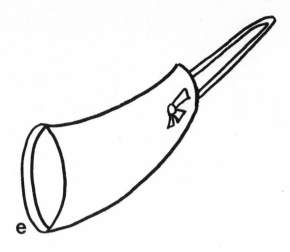

Hat

Make a fairly tight plait with three strands of raffia. Using matching thread, oversew edges in a coil, gradually shaping to fit head (Figs 25a and b). Plait the other three strands of raffia rather looser and continue stitching to form brim. When you reach the end of the plait, neaten by knotting the three ends, tuck these under and stitch very neatly and strongly.

Horn

Cut a piece of adhesive tape slightly longer than edge of cardboard. Place the edge of cardboard along the centre of tape, sticking one edge. Now place the edge of the second piece of cardboard along the centre of tape (Fig 25c). Turn the end of tape over to neaten. Cut another piece of tape and join the other two edges. You will now have a cardboard horn. Oversew the two edges of blue felt horn pieces together. Turn. Slip over the cardboard (Fig 25d). Thread a needle with a 10 in (25·4 cm) length of raffia, and make a knot in the end. Push needle through end of horn where marked on pattern. Pass through to other side, and make a knot to enable horn to hang round neck (Fig 25e).

A FROG HE WOULD A-WOOING GO

A frog he would a-wooing go,
"Hey ho!" said Rowley,
Whether his mother would let him or
   no,
"Hey ho" said Anthony Rowley!

Patterns pp 120–122.

A FROG HE WOULD A-WOOING GO

Height 18 in (45·7 cm).

MATERIALS

Felt, brown, 16 in × 17½ in (40·6 cm × 44·5 cm) for legs, coat, hat, top of head, buttons and stick.
Felt, yellow, 10 in × 8 in (25·4 cm × 20·3 cm) for waist-coat and lower face.
Felt, white, 4 in (10·2 cm) square, for gloves.
Felt, purple, 3 in × 1 in (7·6 cm × 2·5 cm) for tie.
Felt, flesh-coloured, 3½ in × 3¾ in (8·9 cm × 9·5 cm) for mouth.
Felt, orange, 3 in × 5¼ in (7·6 cm × 13·3 cm) for roses and tie spots.
Felt, green, 4 in × 3 in (10·2 cm × 7·6 cm) for stems.
Felt, gold and black, for eyes.
White embroidery cotton.
Strong cotton material, 24 in × 6 in (61 cm × 15·2 cm) for body.
12 in (30·5 cm) thick wire.
Five pipe cleaners.
Stuffing.

CUT

All pieces according to pattern, plus a strip of brown felt 12 in × 1 in (30·5 cm × 2·5 cm) for stick.

MAKING UP

Oversew the seams in brown head piece, placing A to A, etc, (Fig 26a). Oversew the seams in yellow head piece to match. Press seams with thumbnail. Fold mouth piece in half. Oversew one half to brown upper mouth and half to yellow lower mouth from S to S. Oversew back of head from C to C. Turn to right side. Stuff to a good round shape. Stabstitch from C to S both sides, and round mouth ⅛ in (3 mm) from edge. Stabstitch edges of mouth together from S to B (Fig 26b).

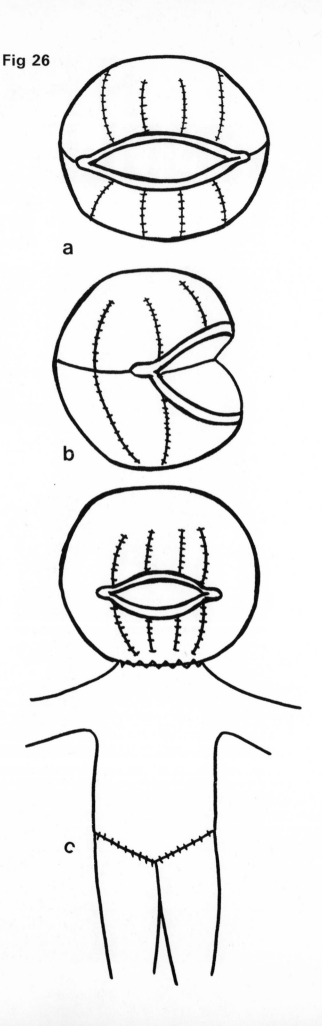

Fig 26

a

b

c

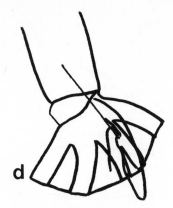

Body

Machine- or backstitch all round body except neck. Turn, press and stuff. Make a narrow under-turning and hem to underside of yellow head piece.

Legs

Place two pieces of leg together and stabstitch from A to B. Consult pattern and stabstitch toes. Cover five small pieces of pipe cleaner with a little stuffing and push one in each toe slot. Put more stuffing into foot and leg, gradually closing the side from B to C. Hem the top of leg to body (Fig 26c). Ladderstitch the gusset at ankle to make foot stand flat (Fig 26d). Make other leg and stitch to body in the same way, making sure the division for toes is opposite.

Fig 27

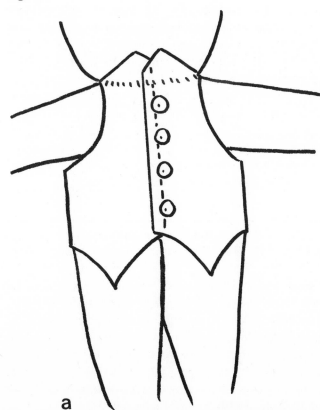

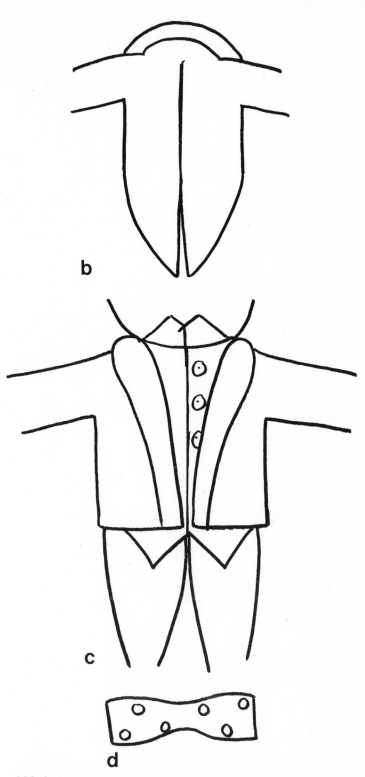

Waistcoat

Hem side edge of right waistcoat piece to body ½ in (1·3 cm) to the back of body side seam. Hem the arm-hole to body. Hem front seam ½ in (1·3 cm) over centre front. Hem the left side of waistcoat to match, over-lapping the right front with centre front. Cut four ⅜ in (1 cm) brown felt circles and hem to front for buttons (Fig 27a). Stitch the stand-up collar in place at neck seam line.

Coat

Oversew the two pieces of back from A to B (Fig 27b). Oversew the fronts to back from C to D and E to F. Beginning ½ in (1·3 cm) from the neck, lightly stitch the back seam of jacket to the back of frog body. Put the frog's arms through sleeves. Stitch the side seams of jacket to waistcoat in line with seam on leg. Turn the edges of jacket over neatly all round fronts to form collar and stitch (Fig 27c). Stitch the two edges of bow tie together for ½ in (1·3 cm) in the middle. Cut six small orange circles with a leather punch and hem to bow (Fig 27d). Stitch bow to neck just under points of waistcoat.

Gloves

Stabstitch the outline of fingers as in pattern. Cut four small pieces of pipe cleaner. Turn one end under and squeeze tightly (Fig 28a). Push this end into finger. Finish other fingers in the same way. Push stuffing into palm and stitch glove to end of arm. Cut round fingers on gloves (Fig 28b and c). Make the other glove in the same way and hem to end of other arm.

Fig 28

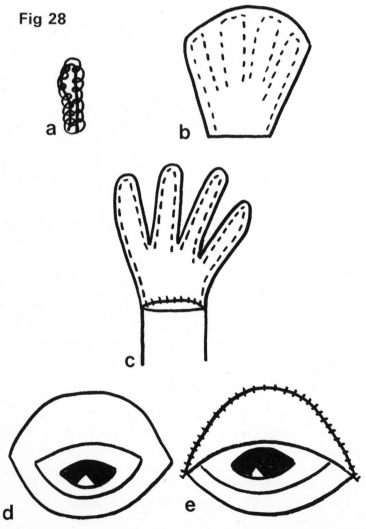

Eyes

Hem black pupil on the centre of gold eye piece. Embroider a white highlight with a few stitches of white thread. Hem the gold eye piece on to the lower edge of brown eye piece (Fig 28d). Oversew the half circle eye piece to the top half of eye on the wrong side (Fig 28e). Turn to right side and stuff. Hem completed eye to top and side of head. Make another eye in the same way, and hem to opposite side of head (Fig 28f).

Hat

Oversew the side seam of hat from A to B. Oversew crown to hat matching the As. Turn to right side and stuff. Oversew the two brim pieces together round outer edge, leaving a small opening from B to C for turning. Turn to right side and ladderstitch opening. Stabstitch round brim ⅛ in (3 mm) in from edge. Stabstitch crown to brim leaving ½ in (1·3 cm) brim all round. Stitch hat to head between the eyes (Fig 29a).

Stick

Turn one end of wire over for 1½ in (3·8 cm). Fold felt strip round wire and stabstitch (Fig 29b).

Flowers

Beginning at A, roll the flower into a coil. Hem the edge to keep firm. Run a thread round the lower part of flower (Fig 29c). Cut a 2 in (5 cm) piece of pipe cleaner and push one end into centre of flower for stalk. Draw the thread to tighten and fasten off, taking a few stitches through pipe cleaner. Fold one of the green stem pieces round pipe cleaner and starting at A stabstitch to the two Bs. Arrange the top to form two leaves around the flower (Fig 29d). Make four more flowers in this manner, and wind a length of green thread round stems to make a bunch.

Place flowers in one hand of frog. If you fold the fingers round the stems, he will hold them. Fold fingers of the other hand round the handle of walking stick, and he will stand quite easily using stick as support.

Fig 29

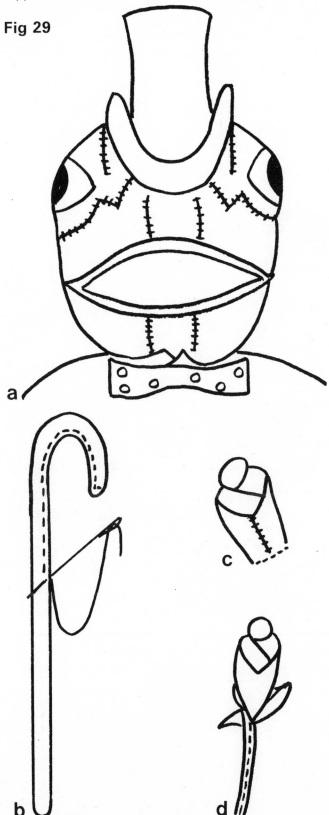

HUMPTY DUMPTY

Humpty Dumpty sat on a wall,
Humpty Dumpty had a great fall.
All the King's horses and all the King's
   men
Couldn't put Humpty together again.

Patterns pp 123–131.

HUMPTY DUMPTY

Height 13 in (33 cm).

MATERIALS

Felt, 9½ in × 17 in (24 cm × 43 cm) flesh-coloured;
12 in × 1 in (30·5 cm × 2·5 cm) purple; 8½ in × 4½ in
(21·6 cm × 11·4 cm) turquoise.
Small pieces red, blue, white, black and brown.
Stranded cotton, red.
Kapok.
22 in × 5 in (56 cm × 12·7 cm) sateen or strong cotton
material for body.

CUT

Two head and two hand pieces from flesh-coloured
felt. One jacket back, placing dotted line to fold of
purple felt.

Two jacket fronts from purple felt, and one piece 1 in ×
2½ in (2·5 cm × 6·4 cm) for bow.

Two trouser pieces from turquoise felt.

Two boots, two soles and two eye pieces from black
felt.

One collar piece, placing pattern to fold of white felt.

Two white eye pieces and two small highlights.

Lips in red felt, eyes in blue and eyebrows in brown.

Two body pieces, with dotted line placed to fold of
sateen.

MAKING UP

Head

Take one of the head pieces and place As together.
Oversew on wrong side to inner A, thus making a dart.
In the same way, continue all round joining Bs, Cs, and
so on. To flatten seam, place thumb nail at inner point
and firmly drag along join to end (Fig 30a). Complete
the other half of head in exactly the same way. Now
place the two halves together, right sides facing, and

matching darts. Oversew all round except between Xs,
which is left open for stuffing. Turn to right side and
flatten seam. Using pattern as a guide, make ears by
stabstitching on right side along dotted lines (Fig 30b),
and at the same time easing in a little stuffing between
the two layers of felt. Stuff head very firmly. Ladderstitch the opening.

Fig 30

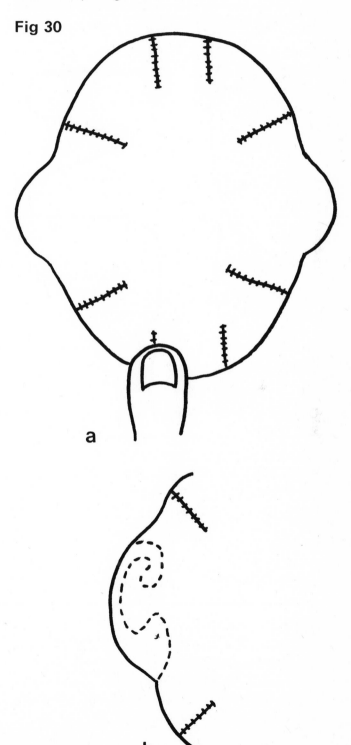

a

b

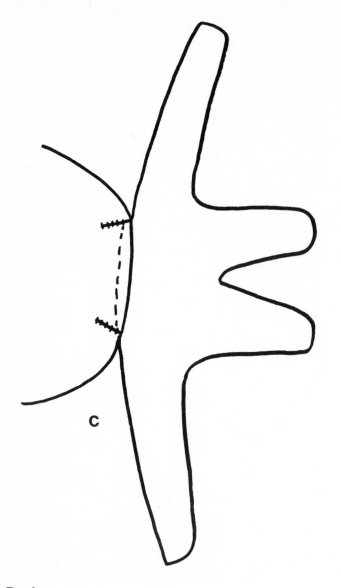

c

Body

Place two body pieces together and machine or back-stitch all round except between As. Turn to right side and stuff. Hem to head between Xs (Fig 30c).

Trousers

Oversew the short front and back seams. Stitch inner leg seams. Flatten seams. Turn to right side and put on doll. Hem to body just under arms (Figure 31a).

Boots

Fold boot in half and oversew from A to B. Oversew boot to sole on wrong side. Turn to right side and stuff firmly to within $\frac{1}{4}$ in (6 mm) of top. Push trouser leg up out of the way and hem boot in place on leg. Make second boot in the same way (Fig 31b).

Features

Hem white highlight to black eye circle. Hem this to blue eye circle. Then hem the whole to the white eye

shape (Fig 31c). Now hem the eye on the face. I think it is a good idea to make both eyes and then lay all the features on the face to get an idea of the whole appearance before actually stitching. Be sure to keep the features well down on the face for a youthful look. The bottom of the eyes should be level with the bottom of the ears. Hem the lips in place in the centre $\frac{1}{8}$ in (3 mm) below the eyes. Hem the brows $\frac{1}{2}$ in (1·3 cm) above the eyes. Embroider a nose taking two small stitches with red embroidery thread (Fig 31d).

Jacket

Oversew the shoulder, sleeve and side seams of jacket. Press. Turn to right side. Put on and hem to doll round neck and for one inch (2·5 cm) down centre front. Hem the collar to neck just above jacket edge, keeping it firm on shoulders. Fold the bow in half length-ways. Oversew the centre for $\frac{1}{2}$ in (1·3 cm). Open ends and press centre flat (Figs 31e and f). Stitch to neck at centre collar.

Hands

Fold hands in half. Oversew all round except lower edge. Turn and stuff firmly to within $\frac{1}{4}$ in (6 mm) of top. Push coat sleeve up and hem hand to arm, making sure the thumb is on top.

Fig 31

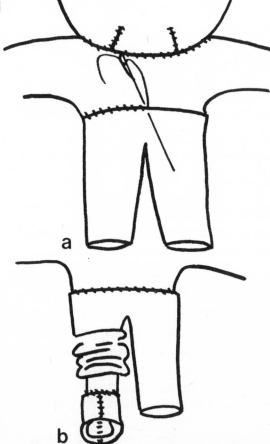

a

b

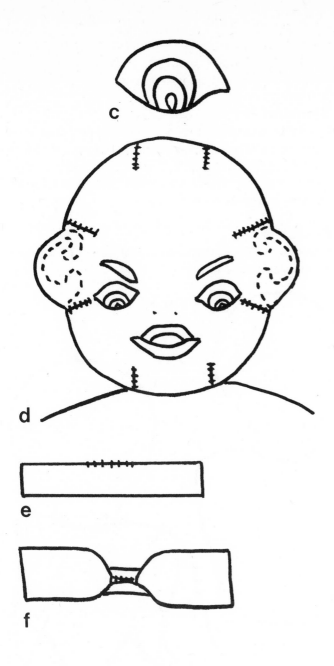

Narrow red braid, 9 in (23 cm).
Narrow gold braid, 3½ in (9 cm).
Embroidery cotton, black, brown, white, gold and red.
Cardboard.

CUT

From flesh-coloured felt, two head pieces, two body pieces, four legs, two straight arm and two bent arm pieces.

Four glove pieces in white felt, two shoe uppers in black felt, and four sole pieces in chamois leather.

Two bearskin pieces in fur fabric, one trouser piece in black felt. Two jacket pieces in red felt for the front, and one piece, placing straight edge of pattern to fold of material, for back.

MAKING UP

Oversew head pieces together all round, leaving neck between A and B open for stuffing. Turn and stuff firmly. Place on one side. Oversew body pieces together all round, leaving neck between A and B open for stuffing. Turn and stuff very firmly. Ladderstitch opening. Ladderstitch head to body (Fig 33a).

Legs

Oversew all round legs except top. Turn and stuff very firmly. Stitch to doll as marked on pattern.

Fig 32

GUARDSMAN

Height 8½ in (21·6 cm).

MATERIALS

Felt, flesh-coloured, 10 in × 7 in (25·4 cm × 17·8 cm) for doll.
Felt, black, 7½ in × 4 in (19 cm × 10·2 cm).
Felt, red, 7¾ in × 7 in (19·7 cm × 17·8 cm).
Felt, white, small piece for gloves and belt.
Chamois leather for soles.
Kapok.
Fur fabric, black, 5½ in × 2¼ in (14 cm × 5·7 cm).

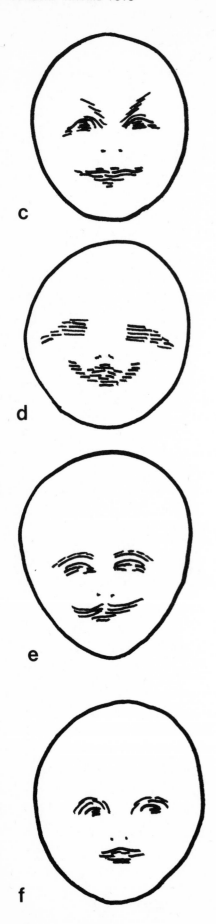

c

d

e

f

Arms

Oversew all round except top. Turn and stuff very firmly. Stitch to body in desired position (Fig 33b).

Bearskin

Place the two pieces of the bearskin together right sides facing. Oversew with long stitches from A to B to C. Make a backstitch seam $\frac{1}{4}$ in (6 mm) in from edge. Turn. Stuff top. Turn under edge and hem to head, bringing it well down at the back.

Features

Embroider features as shown in Figs 32c or choose any of the expressions in Figs 32a–f.

Fig 33

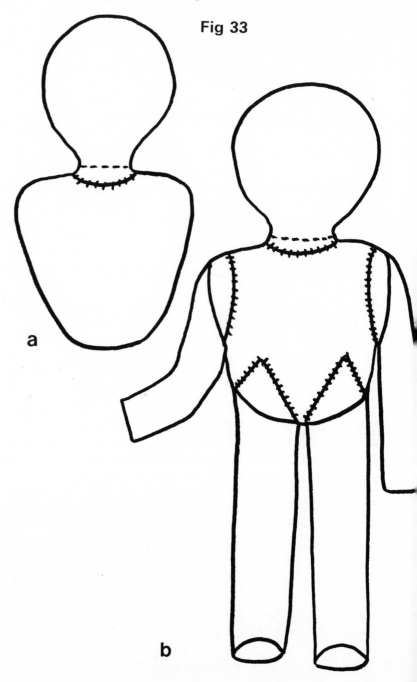

a

b

c

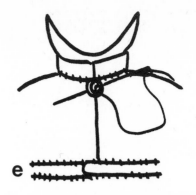

e

Trousers

Stitch red braid on right side as shown by dotted line on pattern. Fold trousers in half. On wrong side, oversew from A to B. Now fold Bs to C and oversew the leg seams. Turn. Hem to doll at waist. Turn up lower edges of trousers to enable you to stitch shoes to legs.

Shoes

Oversew two pieces of chamois leather together from C to B to C. Turn to right side. Slip cardboard sole between. Turn ends in and stitch neatly. Oversew the front seam of the uppers. Place the seam to centre front of sole on wrong side and oversew all round. Turn and put on doll. Stitch the centre top of shoe to the centre of foot. Fold each side to centre, so that the top fits the ankle, and take four stitches down front. Stitch the top of shoe to leg. Turn down trouser leg over top of shoe (Figs 34a and b).

Fig 34

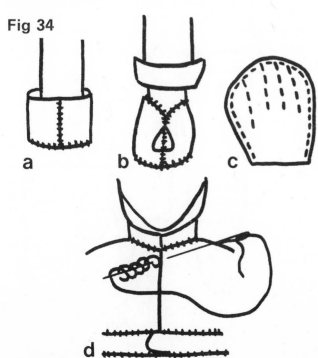

a   b   c

d

Jacket

Oversew shoulder seams from A to B, and side seams from C to D. Cut a strip of red felt $\frac{1}{4}$ in (6 mm) wide to fit neck edge. Oversew to neck edge on wrong side for collar. Turn to right side and put on doll. Hem right side of jacket to doll, beginning at neck edge and continuing for 2 in (5 cm) down centre front. Hem left side over this. Cut a strip of white felt $\frac{1}{4}$ in (6 mm) wide and hem to waist (both edges) for belt.

Gloves

Place two glove pieces together and stabstitch all round except top. Put a little stuffing inside. Stabstitch as shown in Fig 34c to form fingers. Place a little more stuffing in for palm. Turn up end of sleeve and hem to arm all the way round, making sure the thumb A is on top.

Stitch the gold braid each side of head under the edge of bearskin. Keep in place by taking a few stitches under the chin.

Make three buttons from collar to belt in the following way: thread a large crewel needle with one strand of gold embroidery cotton. Put the needle in just under the collar, centre front. Take two small stitches to fasten. Now put the needle in again in the same spot. Wind the thread 12 times round the needle (Fig 34d). Push needle right through and take another stitch underneath the ring formed by the previous stitch (Fig 34e). Put the needle in again at the same spot and bring up halfway between newly made button and the belt. Make another button here as before, and another one just above belt.

CAVALRY SOLDIER

Fig 35

Height 9 in (23 cm).

MATERIALS

Felt, flesh-coloured, 10 in × 7 in (25·4 cm × 17·8 cm) for doll.
Felt, white, 5½ in × 6¼ in (14 cm × 16 cm) and four pieces 1½ in × 2½ in (3·8 cm × 6·4 cm).
Felt, grey, 2¾ in × 6 in (7 cm × 15·2 cm).
Felt, black, four pieces 3½ in × 2½ in (9 cm × 6·4 cm).
Felt, red, 5¾ in × 7 in (14·6 cm × 17·8 cm).
Felt, gold, small pieces.
Chamois leather for soles.
Kapok.
Narrow gold braid, 9 in (23 cm).
Embroidery cotton, black, red and gold.
Extra strong button thread, 8 yards (7·32 m).
Cardboard.

CUT

From Guardsman pattern and in flesh-coloured felt, head, body, legs and four straight arm pieces.

Helmet back, front and two peaks in grey felt, jacket (as for Guardsman) in red, and four boots in black.

Trousers, four gloves, one belt and a sash 6 in × ¼ in (15·2 cm × 6 mm), all in white felt.

Collar, helmet trim and two shoulder tabs in gold felt.

MAKING UP

Doll

Make exactly the same as Guardsman, but with two straight arms.

Features

Work features as in Fig 32b.

Helmet

Place two pieces of peak together and oversew from B to C to B. Turn. Flatten seam. Matching Bs, oversew peak to helmet front, working through three thicknesses of felt. Press seam flat. Oversew helmet front to helmet back, starting at top A, down right side to B, then A down left side to B. Turn. Press seam. Put a little stuffing in top. Starting at right side, stitch yellow braid round helmet; do not cut end (Figs 35a and b). Put on doll, making sure the peak is in the centre of front. Pass the yellow braid under chin, catch with a few stitches to keep in place, and take up the other side of face. Fasten off neatly to match right side (Fig 35c).

back

a

b

c

d

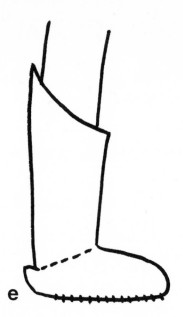

e

Helmet trim

Wind the thread round a piece of cardboard $3\frac{1}{2}$ in (9 cm) long (Fig 36d). Tie top with cotton. Cut the other end to form tassel (Fig 36e). Wind a length of embroidery cotton six times round tassel $\frac{1}{2}$ in (1·3 cm) from top. Neatly tie to secure (Fig 36f). Roll the small piece of felt round top of tassel and hem to secure. Attach the tassel to the felt with a few stitches (Fig 36g). Hem the tassel to centre top of helmet. Bend the strands of tassel downwards. If they will not readily bend, dampen with a little water and gently stroke over and down (Fig 36h).

Trousers

Make as for Guardsman, omitting braid stripes. Put on doll and stitch to waist. Stitch lower trouser leg to body (Fig 35d).

Boots

Make a pair of soles as for Guardsman. Oversew two pieces of boot from A to B and from C to D. Place the front seam of boot to the centre front of sole, on wrong side, and oversew all round. Turn and put on doll. Stitch to ankle as marked on pattern, to form a spur from E to B (Fig 35e).

Jacket

Oversew shoulder and side seams as for Guardsman. Thread a fine needle with one strand of black embroidery cotton and chain stitch along the centre of collar, leaving $\frac{1}{8}$ in (3 mm) each side of end. Oversew collar to neck of jacket on wrong side. Turn to right side and put on doll. Hem right side of jacket to body of doll, just over half way down centre front. Hem left side over this. Make a belt as for Guardsman and finish

with embroidered buckle, using one strand of gold embroidery cotton (Fig 36a). Make six buttons from collar to belt as for Guardsman. Embroider a line along centre of shoulder tabs as you did the collar. Lay the shoulder tab right side to jacket at the end of shoulder so that when it is turned to right side, the edge will come just against the collar. Hem in place. Turn over and fasten at neck edge with one button made in the same way as front buttons (Figs 36b and c). Hem the ends of sleeves to lower arms, easing where necessary. The sash should measure from under the right arm just above belt, across front to felt shoulder tab, and across back to join up at right underarm. Thread fine needle with one strand of red embroidery cotton, and chain stitch along the centre of sash. Put on doll, passing through the left shoulder tab and stitch neatly under right arm.

Gloves

Place two pieces together and oversew from A round fingers to B. Turn and press seam with thumbnail. Put a little stuffing inside and stabstitch to form fingers as the guide on pattern. Put a little more stuffing in to form palm. Put on doll, making sure thumb A is on top. Stitch to end of arm at wrist.

Fig 36

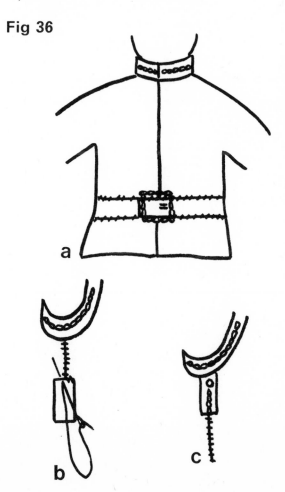

a

b

c

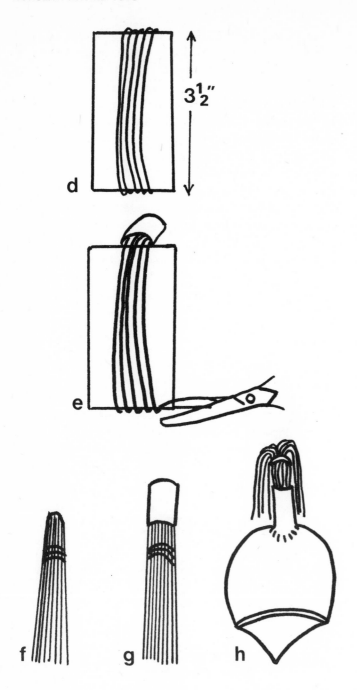

HIGHLAND REGIMENT SOLDIER

Height 7½ in (19 cm).

MATERIALS

Felt, flesh-coloured, 10 in × 7 in (25·4 cm × 17·8 cm) for doll.

Felt, navy blue, 11½ in × 2¾ in (29·2 cm × 6·5 cm) for jacket. Felt, black, two pieces 2¼ in × 1¼ in (5·7 cm × 3·2 cm), one piece 1½ in × 1¾ in (3·8 cm × 4·5 cm) and two pieces 3½ in × 1¼ in (9 cm × 3·2 cm).

Tartan material for trews, 6 in × 4½ in (15·2 cm × 11·4 cm).

Brown leather for sash, 5¼ in × ¼ in (13·3 cm × 6 mm).

Brown leather for belt, 5 in × ¼ in (12·7 cm × 6 mm).

Brown leather or felt for gloves.

Small red-and-white-check cotton for hat edge.

Black ribbon, 3 in × ½ in (7·6 cm × 1·3 cm).

Short lengths of embroidery cotton, grey, brown, white and red, for features and buttons.

Kapok.

Chamois leather for soles.

CUT

Doll as for Guardsman, with one straight arm and one bent.

Two jacket fronts and one jacket back in navy felt. Trews from Guardsman pattern in tartan. Make sure the pattern on each leg is exactly the same.

Two Glengarry hat pieces, one Glengarry crown and shoes as for Guardsman in black felt.

MAKING UP

Make in the same way as Guardsman, as far as arms.

Fig 37

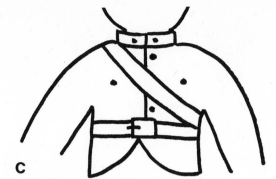

C

Features

Work as in Fig 32c; brown eyes, brows and moustache, red nose and lower lip.

Hat

Oversew the crown to one of the sides from A to B. Oversew other side to match. Oversew from A to D and B to C. Put on head, leaning slightly to the right side. Hem all round the head. Now with single strand of brown cotton take several long and short stitches on each side and at the back of head for hair. Cut a length of red check material $\frac{1}{2}$ in (1·3 cm) wide. Turn ends under and pin to head so that it trims the edge of hat. Hem all round. Fold the black ribbon in half, with one end $\frac{1}{2}$ in (1·3 cm) longer than the other. Stitch to back of head just under the centre back of hat. Cut the ends of ribbon to a point in centre (Figs 37a and b).

Trews

Make as for Guardsman's trousers without braid. Make a small hem at the end of each leg. Turn the waist edge under, and stitch to body.

Shoes

Make these the same as for Guardsman and stitch to legs.

Jacket

Oversew shoulder and side seams. Cut a strip of navy felt $\frac{1}{4}$ in (6 mm) wide and oversew to neck edge for collar. Turn to right side and put on doll. Hem right side of jacket to doll from neck to shaped lower edge. Hem the left front over this. Embroider three grey buttons from neck to $\frac{1}{4}$ in (6 mm) above shaped jacket front. Embroider a grey button each side of centre one, and make two small french knots for trimming on front of collar. Stitch end of sash under left arm, take over right shoulder and stitch under arm on top of first end. Stitch one end of belt to jacket under button and above front shaping, take round body and fasten at front with a grey embroidered buckle (Fig 37c).

Gloves

Make as for Guardsman.

11TH HUSSARS OFFICER 1900

Height 9 in (23 cm).

MATERIALS

Felt, flesh-coloured, 10 in × 7 in (25·4 cm × 17·8 cm) for doll.
Felt, maroon, 7$\frac{1}{2}$ in × 4 in (19 cm × 10·2 cm) and 4 in × 1 in (10·2 cm × 2·5 cm).
Felt, grey, 7$\frac{3}{4}$ in × 7 in (19·7 cm × 17·8 cm).
Felt, white, 2 pieces 1$\frac{1}{2}$ in × 2$\frac{1}{2}$ in (3·8 cm × 6·4 cm).
Black felt for shoes.
Scraps of maroon.
Chamois leather for soles.
Black fur fabric for busby, 6 in × 2$\frac{1}{4}$ in (15·2 cm × 5·7 cm).
Narrow gold braid, 21 in (53·3 cm).
Kapok.
Embroidery cotton, grey to match felt, and brown for features.
White button thread, 27 in (68·6 cm).

CUT

Doll as for Guardsman.

Trousers in maroon felt, as for Guardsman.

Jacket in grey felt, as for Guardsman.

Gloves in white felt as for Guardsman.

Two busby pieces in fur fabric.

Shoes as for Guardsman.

MAKING UP

Doll

Make in the same way as Guardsman, as far as arms.

Busby

Place two pieces of busby together, right sides facing. Oversew with long stitches from A to B to C. Make a backstitch seam $\frac{1}{4}$ in (6 mm) in from edge. Turn and stuff top. Turn under edge and hem to head. Stitch narrow braid round the bottom (Fig 38a). Fold a piece of maroon felt in half, and stitch to busby in position (Fig 38a). Wind the white button thread round a piece of card 1$\frac{1}{2}$ in (3·8 cm) long. Tie a thread through one end to keep the strands in position (Fig 38d). Cut the cardboard away. Roll a piece of $\frac{1}{4}$ in (6 mm) maroon felt round the end and stitch firm (Fig 38e).

Cut through the top strands and trim neatly. Stitch to busby at centre top (Fig 38a).

Fig 38

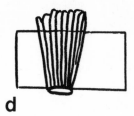

d

e

a

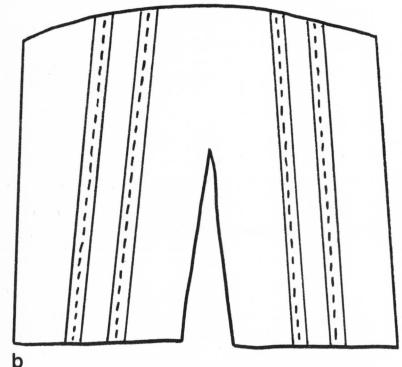

b

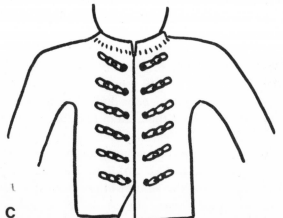

c

Features

Embroider as in Fig 32d.

Trousers

Make up and stitch trousers to body as for Guardsman, but stitch two rows of braid on outside of each leg (Fig 38b).

Shoes

Make and stitch to doll as for Guardsman.

Jacket

Make jacket in grey felt as for Guardsman. Turn to right side and put on doll. Hem right side of jacket to doll from neck 1¾ in (4·5 cm) down centre front. Hem left side over this. Now, using the full thickness of embroidery cotton, make a French knot and three chain stitches each side of centre front. This is the button and braid trimming. Repeat this five more times (Fig 38c).

Gloves

Make in white felt as for Guardsman's hands, and stitch to arm.

QUEEN'S 'ROYAL WEST SURREY REGIMENT' SERGEANT 1881

Height 8¾ in (22 cm).

MATERIALS

Felt, flesh-coloured, 10 in × 7 in (25·4 cm × 17·8 cm) for doll.
Felt, navy blue, 10½ in × 5 in (26·7 cm × 12·7 cm).
Felt, red, 8 in × 6 in (20·3 cm × 15·2 cm).
Felt, white, 6¼ in × ½ in (1·3 cm × 16 cm).
Felt, gold, small piece.
Gold braid, 3½ in (9 cm).
Black leather, 4 in (10·2 cm) square.
Embroidery cotton, white, red, gold and brown.

CUT

Doll as for Guardsman (except for shoes), with one straight arm and one bent.

One trouser piece, two cuffs, two helmet pieces, two helmet peaks and one collar ¼ in × 3¼ in (6 mm × 8·3 cm) in navy blue felt.

Two jacket pieces and two shoulder tabs in red felt.

One piece of helmet trim in gold felt.

Two pairs of boot pieces in black leather, and two cardboard soles.

MAKING UP

Doll
Make in the same way as Guardsman, as far as arms.

Fig 39

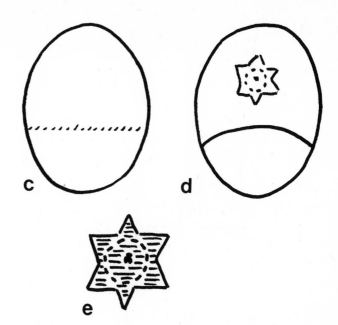

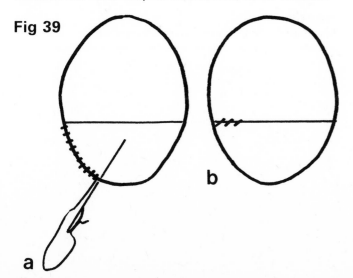

Helmet
Place one piece of helmet peak on top of one piece of helmet at dotted line. Oversew from A to B to A (Fig 39a). Turn to right side. Now, on inside, hem the straight edge of peak to helmet from A to A (Fig 39b). Stitch other pieces to match. Place two pieces of helmet together, right sides facing, and oversew from A to C to A (Fig 39c). Turn to right side. Embroider badge on centre front with one strand of gold embroidery cotton. In the centre of the badge make a French knot and circle it with backstitch, using one strand of red embroidery cotton (Figs 39d and e). Put a little stuffing in the top of helmet. Stitch the braid under one side, and put helmet on doll. Stitch the braid down side of face, under chin and up the other side. Finish neatly on inside of helmet.

Features
Embroider these as Fig 32e, the moustache, eyes and brows in brown, the highlight in white.

Trousers
Fold trousers in half, right side inside. Oversew from A to B. Now fold Cs to Ds and oversew the leg seams. Stitch the small pleats in the waistband.

Boots
Oversew boots all round, except the top. Turn to right side. Place a cardboard sole in the bottom of boot and put on doll. Hem boot to doll round top. Place the bottom of trouser legs, wrong side outside, over the boots. Hem to boots just below the top, easing as necessary (Fig 40a). Pull trousers up and hem to waist, making a small pleat each side of front and back (Fig 40b).

Fig 40

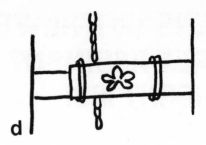

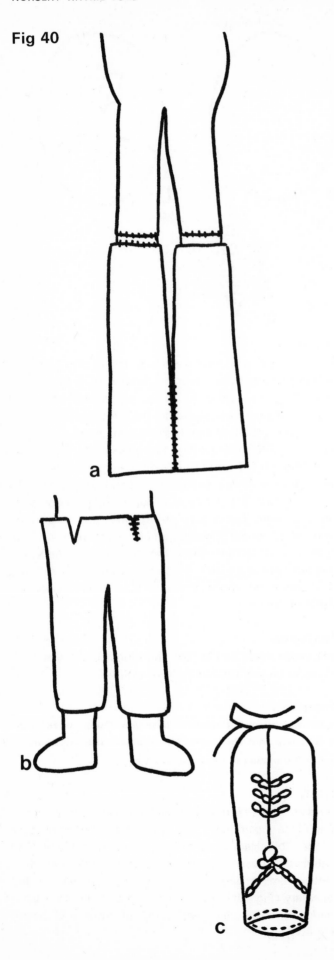

Jacket

Cut one piece in half to form two front pieces. Oversew shoulder and side seams as for Guardsman. Embroider three small gold lazy daisy stitches each end of collar. Oversew collar to neck edge of jacket on wrong side. Stitch the cuffs over ends of sleeves with the point A on top sleeve seam. Use tiny running stitches on lower edge and hem the upper edge. With three strands of white embroidery cotton, chain stitch along the upper cuff seam, working three lazy daisy stitches at the top of the point. With four strands of gold embroidery cotton, work three stripes in chain stitch on the right sleeve (Fig 40c). With three strands of white embroidery thread, and beginning at the top of right collar, chain stitch round the collar seam and down the left side of jacket front. Put on doll. Fasten left front over right, and embroider five French knot buttons from collar to waist in gold. Using three strands of white, chain stitch all round shoulder tab. Stitch the point to collar edge on sleeve seam line, and hem the other end on shoulder edge. Finish with a gold French knot button in centre of point. Embroider five lazy daisy stitches in gold $\frac{1}{2}$ in (1·3 cm) in from end of belt (Fig 40d). Place belt round doll with the embroidered buckle end overlapping on top. Take four long stitches over width of belt on each side of buckle.

Roll helmet trim quite tight. Bind with matching cotton a little way in from one end. Hem this to the centre top of helmet.

Hands

Make and stitch to arm as for Guardsman.

TROOPER 21ST LANCERS 1914

Height 8 in (20 cm).

MATERIALS

Felt, flesh-coloured, 10 in × 7 in (25·4 cm × 17·8 cm) for doll.
Felt, navy blue, 8½ in × 9 in (21·6 cm × 23 cm).
Felt, pale blue, 4½ in × 2 in (11·4 cm × 5 cm).
Small pieces white, red and gold felt.
Black leather, 7 in × 3 in (17·8 cm × 7·6 cm) for boots.
Gold braid, 18 in.
Kapok.
Embroidery cotton, black, white, red and gold.

CUT

Doll as for Guardsman.

Gloves in white felt, belt in red felt, collar and shoulder tabs in pale blue felt, all as for Cavalry soldier.

One jacket back, one right front, one left front, two trouser pieces, two helmet pieces and two helmet peaks, all in navy blue felt.

One overfront piece in pale blue felt.

One semi-circular helmet trim in gold felt and three rectangular pieces of helmet trim in pale blue felt.

Two pairs of boot pieces in black leather.

MAKING UP

Doll

Make in the same way as Guardsman, as far as arms.

Features

Work as in Fig 32f, eyes in black and white, brows in black, mouth and nose in red.

Fig 41

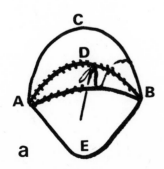

Helmet

Place one helmet peak to helmet, matching As, Bs and Es. Oversew from A to B. Turn to right side and hem loose edge of peak to helmet. Stitch other piece of helmet and peak to match. On wrong side, oversew two pieces of helmet together from A to C to B. This forms the crown. Turn to right side. Hem the piece of gold trim to front of helmet above peak (Fig 41a). Put a little stuffing in crown of helmet. Put on doll. Stitch one end of braid strap to outside of side of helmet. Continue stitching down side of face, under chin and up other side of face, finishing on other side of helmet. With one strand of gold embroidery cotton, join two pieces of pale blue helmet trim together from G to H, using blanket stitch (Fig 41b). Now take third pale blue piece and in the same way stitch each edge to the edge of the previous piece, thus forming a triangle. Work in the same stitch round the top, and attach to helmet (Fig 41c). Make a tassel as for Cavalry Soldier and stitch to inside of helmet trim on left side.

Trousers

Oversew side seams of trousers from A to B. Oversew inner leg seams. Turn to right side. Stitch a braid stripe on each side of outside leg seam, from waist to lower leg. Put on doll. Hem to doll at waist and legs, easing where necessary.

Boots

Oversew the two pieces of boot together all round, except top. Turn and press the seam with thumbnail to flatten. Cut two cardboard soles as for (RWSR) sergeant and put one in each boot. Put boots on doll.

Jacket

Oversew shoulder, sleeve and side seams. Turn to right side. Tack the pale blue front to left front of jacket. Starting at centre front, oversew the collar through both thicknesses along left side, and across back to right shoulder. Put on doll. Hem right front to doll. Hem the navy blue left front over right front. Stitch the pale blue front to shoulder seam on both sides. Finish stitching collar to jacket, meeting at centre front. Make a French knot button on each side of centre front collar. Fasten the blue front to navy blue with five gold French knot buttons on each side (Fig 41d). Using one strand of gold embroidery thread, chain stitch all round edge of shoulder tabs. Hem shoulder tabs to shoulder edge of jacket. Fasten at neck edge with a gold French knot button. Hem the scarlet belt round waist, joining under right arm. Using one strand of embroidery thread, chain stitch round top and lower edge of belt. Make a third row of chain stitching round centre of belt. Using one strand of pale blue embroidery thread, chain stitch along lower edge and open edge of jacket.

Gloves

Oversew from A round fingers to B. Turn and press seam with thumbnail. Put a little stuffing inside and stabstitch to form fingers as shown on pattern. Put on doll, with A on top. Stitch to doll firmly round wrist.

SIMPLE SIMON

Simple Simon met a pieman going to the fair,
Said Simple Simon to the pieman "Let me taste your ware".
Said the pieman to Simple Simon "Show me first your penny",
Said Simple Simon to the pieman "Sir, I have not any!"

Patterns pp 132–147.

PIEMAN

Height 17 in (43 cm).

MATERIALS

Felt, flesh-coloured, 26 in × 8 in (66 cm × 20·3 cm) for doll.
Dark brown crêpe hair, 12 in (30·5 cm).
Small pieces felt, white, brown and black.
Pipe cleaners.
Stuffing.
Adhesive tape.
Wood, 5 in × ½ in (12·7 cm × 1·3 cm) diameter.
Embroidery cotton, strands of brown, red and white.
White calico, 36 in × 18 in (91·4 cm × 45·7 cm).
Six linen buttons ½ in (1·3 cm) diameter.
Two linen buttons ⅜ in (1 cm) diameter.
Eleven press studs size 00.
Cardboard for tray, 6 in × 4¼ in (15·2 cm × 10·8 cm).
Black leather for shoes, 5½ in × 3½ in (14 cm × 9 cm).
Brown felt for tray 6 in × 4¼ in (15·2 cm × 10·8 cm); for strap, 15 in × ½ in (38 cm × 1·3 cm).
Gold felt for pies, 12 in × 3 in (30·5 cm × 7·6 cm).
White stockinette for socks, 8 in × 4 in (20·3 cm × 10 cm).
Chamois leather for soles, 3½ in × 6½ in (9 cm × 16·5 cm).

CUT

One head, one face, two body pieces, two soles of foot, two inner and two outer legs, two pairs of arms and two pairs of hands in flesh-coloured felt.

Two eyes in white, brown and black felt.

Two pairs of shoes in black leather, two soles in chamois leather and two in cardboard.

Two coat fronts, two coat backs, two pairs of trouser pieces, one hat, belt 4 in × 1 in (10 cm × 2·5 cm), one collar 5 in × 2 in (12·7 cm × 5 cm), two cuff pieces 4 in × 1¾ in (10 cm × 4·5 cm) and one head band 11 in × 4 in (28 cm × 10 cm), all in calico.

Pie pieces in gold felt.

Two white socks.

MAKING UP

Place two pieces of body together and oversew all round except top A to B. Turn to right side and stuff firmly. Bind piece of wood with adhesive tape. Place half in centre of body. Oversew neck each side of stick.

Fig 42

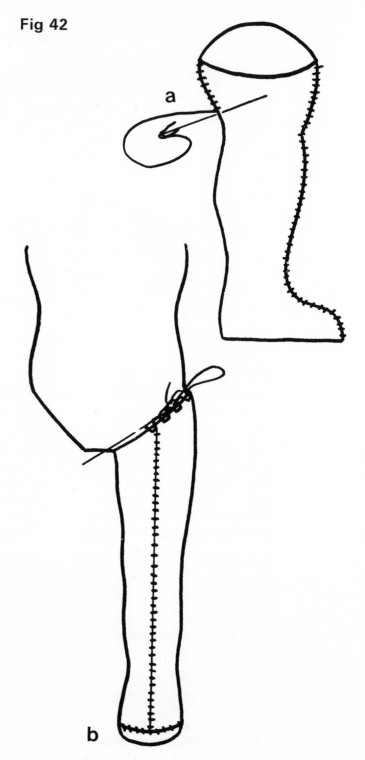

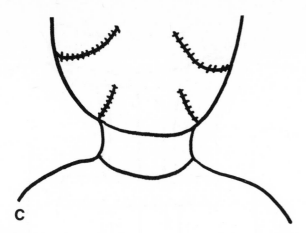

c

Fig 43

a

b

c

d

Legs

Place one outer and one inner leg piece together. Oversew from A to B and C to D (Fig 42a). Oversew the sole piece to lower part of leg matching Bs and Ds. Turn and stuff firmly. Ladderstitch to body at E and F. Make another leg, making sure you reverse the top shaping (Fig 42b). Ladderstitch to body.

Arms

Oversew two arm pieces together all round except between J and H, which is left open for stuffing. Turn. Turn under ends of four pipe cleaners and bind well with stuffing. Push into arms and add small pieces of stuffing until the arms are very firm. The pipe cleaners will help the arms to bend and hold the tray of pies. Ladderstitch the arm to body as shown by dotted line GHJ on pattern.

Hands

Oversew hand all round, leaving wrist open. Bend five small pieces of pipe cleaner in half for fingers and push into hand. Stabstitch between to divide (see pattern). Push a little stuffing into palm and ladderstitch over end of arm. Make other hand to match and stitch to arm.

Head

On face, place C to C and oversew seam. Place D to D and oversew. Continue all round in this way. Stitch seams in back head piece in the same way. Oversew the two head pieces together, matching Cs, Es, Fs and Hs. Turn to right side and stuff firmly. Push the end of wood into head. Ladderstitch the neck of head on top of the neck edge of body, adding more stuffing as necessary to make a very firm neck (Fig 42c).

Hair

Ease the hair sideways and lay across head. Backstitch a seam parting with double flesh-coloured thread. Arrange hair round head, and in a few places, stitch to head on the underside to keep hair in place (Fig 43a).

Features

Hem brown eye piece to white, and then hem black pupil to brown. Hem to face. It is a good idea to make both eyes before attaching to face, and arrange on face until you get the right expression. Embroider thick brown eyebrows with one strand of embroidery cotton. Now make some lines on face by stabstitching the line from eye for one inch thus : put needle in at top of seam, pass under seam and bring out on other side. Take another stitch back again. Continue in this way for one inch (Fig 43b). This will raise the seam line and form a ridge. Make a line on the other side of face in the same way. Consulting Fig 43c, embroider mouth in red. Raise the shape of nose with two wrinkles each side of mouth by stab-stitching in the same way as the cheek wrinkles. Stabstitch outline of ear each side of face (Fig 43d).

Socks

Stitch from A to B. Make a narrow hem round top of sock. Turn and press. Put on doll. Make another sock to match.

Trousers

Join side seams from A to B. Join inner leg seams. Join two leg pieces together. Make a narrow hem on side slit of leg from B to C. Make a ⅜ in (1 cm) hem round lower edge of each leg. Make a ⅜ in (1 cm) hem round top of trousers. Make a ½ in (1·3 cm) pleat each side of front seam. On underside sew four press studs. On top of these, stitch four small linen buttons (Fig 44a). Make a ½ in (1·3 cm) pleat each side of back seam. Sew two press studs on underside. This is a simple way of allowing the trousers to be taken off for washing. Put on doll and fasten.

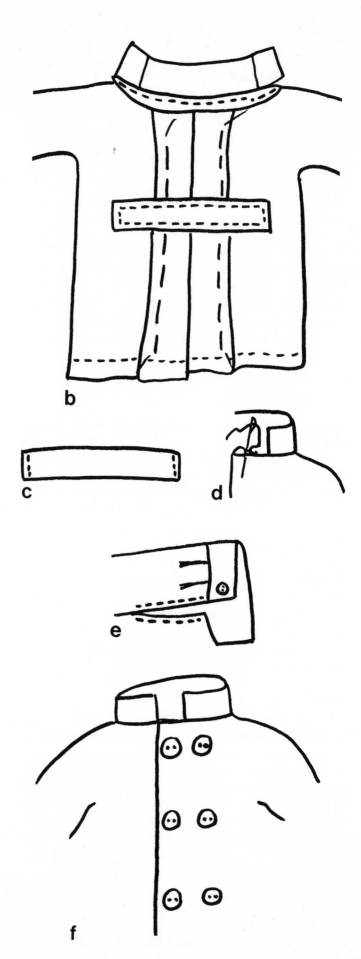

b

c

d

e

f

Fig 44

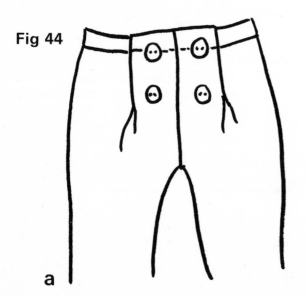

a

Coat

Stitch the sleeve and side seams on each piece from A to B to C. Stitch the top sleeve seam from D to E. Make a 1 in (2·5 cm) hem down each front. Stitch back seam from F to G. Make a hem on each side from H to J. Catch stitch left hem over right hem at G. Make a $\frac{1}{4}$ in (6 mm) pleat each side of centre back from K to J. Tack to hold. Turn under $\frac{1}{4}$ in (6 mm) on edges of belt piece and tack to centre back at G and H. Stitch belt to back of coat. Take out all the tacking stitches. Make a $\frac{1}{2}$ in (1·3 cm) hem on lower edges of coat (Fig 44b). Fold the collar in half lengthwise, and stitch short ends (Fig 44c). Starting in the centre of right front hem, and finishing in the centre of left front hem, stitch collar to neck edge. First lay collar round neck edge, right sides facing, and then stitch one thickness of collar to neck edge (Fig 44b). Now turn to inside and hem other edge of collar on seamline. Turn in the front edges and oversew (Fig 44d). Make a very narrow hem on sleeve edge L to A. Fold cuff in half lengthways and stitch short edges together. Stitch cuff to end of sleeve in the same way that you did the collar, leaving $\frac{1}{2}$ in (1·3 cm) extended on front side and exactly in line with hem on the back of sleeve, and making small pleats to take up the fullness (Fig 44e). Press. Sew a small button on each cuff and a press stud to fasten. Stitch six buttons on front of coat to finish (Fig 44f).

Shoes

Oversew the two chamois leather soles together, leaving CBD open. Turn to right side. Slip cardboard sole between them and ladderstitch opening. Oversew the upper fronts from C to B, and back from D to A on wrong side. Oversew sole to upper on wrong side matching As and Bs. Turn. Put on doll. Make another shoe to match.

Hat

Fold the hat band in half and stitch the seam to make into band (Fig 45a). Fold in half lengthways and press, making a double band. Turn under each edge of band. Pleat the edge of crown to fit band and pin (Fig 45b). With right sides together stitch crown to one thickness of band. Hem the other side of band on seamline (Fig 45c).

Fig 45

Tray

Cut $\frac{1}{2}$ in (1·3 cm) square from each corner of cardboard. Bend on dotted lines (Figs 45d and e) and seal the corners with a little adhesive tape. Cut $\frac{1}{2}$ in (1·3 cm) square from each corner of the brown felt. Oversew the corners. Turn to right side. Slip felt on outside of cardboard tray and secure with a little Copydex. Stitch one end of the strap in the centre of each side of tray. Put round neck of doll.

Pies

Place two pieces of pie together and stabstitch $\frac{1}{4}$ in (6 mm) in from edge, adding a little stuffing in centre (Fig 45f). Make several more pies and place in the pieman's tray.

SIMPLE SIMON

Fig 46

Height 15½ in (40 cm).

MATERIALS

Felt, flesh-coloured, 14½ in (37 cm) square for doll.
Small ball pale honey-coloured crochet cotton for hair.
Embroidery cotton, blue, red, white and brown.
Strong turquoise blue cotton, 17 in × 11 in (43 cm × 28 cm) for pants and hat.
Fine white cotton, 36 in × 9 in (91·5 cm × 23 cm) for blouse.
Purple felt, 12½ in × 10 in (32 cm × 25·5 cm) for jacket.
Chamois leather for soles.
Black leather, 4¾ in × 2 in (12 cm × 5 cm) for shoe uppers and 6 in × 1½ in (15 cm × 4 cm) for hat peak.
White stockinette 6½ in × 3½ in (16·5 cm × 9 cm) for socks.
Three linen buttons, ½ in (1·3 cm) diameter.
5 in (12·7 cm) piece of wood, ¼ in (6 mm) diameter.
Seven press studs size 00.
Adhesive tape.
Stuffing.
Black embroidery cotton for tassel.
Cardboard for soles.
Pipe cleaners.

CUT

In flesh-coloured felt, two headpieces, two body pieces, two inner legs, two outer legs, two soles-of-feet, four arms and four hands.

Four shoe soles in chamois leather.

Two shoe uppers and two cap peaks in black leather.

Two pairs of trouser pieces, hat crown (cut on dotted line on pattern) and hat band 9 in × 2½ in (23 cm × 6·4 cm) in turquoise blue cotton.

Two jacket fronts and one jacket back in purple felt.

Two blouse fronts, one blouse back, two collar pieces, two cuffs, two pockets and a strip for the collar frill ½ in × 16 in (1·3 cm × 40·6 cm) in fine lawn. If this can be cut with a long selvedge it will make a very neat finish.

MAKING UP

Stitch the body, legs, arms and hands in the same way as for the pie-man.

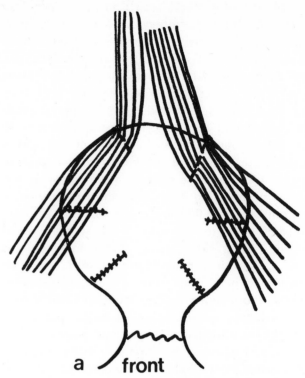

a front

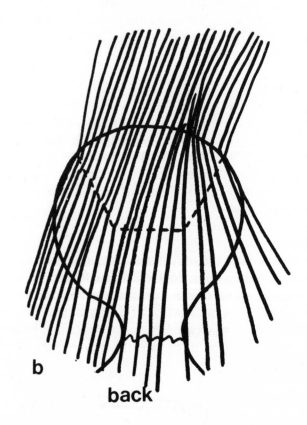

b

back

the rest of hair round head leaving the seam on left side only for parting. Trim hair evenly at back and shape at front (Figs 46c and d).

Features
Consulting Fig 46c and using one strand of embroidery cotton, embroider eyes in white and blue, mouth and nose in red, eyelashes and eyebrows in brown.

Blouse
Stitch shoulder-and-sleeve seams. Stitch underarm and side seams from A to B. Make $\frac{1}{2}$ in (1·3 cm) hem down each front and along lower edge. Make a narrow hem from C to A to C. Fold the cuff in half lengthways and stitch the two short sides. Stitch cuff to sleeve edge, leaving $\frac{1}{4}$ in (6 mm) overlapping on the front edge, and making little tucks each side of opening to take in surplus. Press the blouse. Run a gathering thread along the edge of collar frill. Draw up to fit outer edges of collar from A to B to C to D. Tack to edge of one collar piece, right sides together as in Fig 47a. Place the other side of collar on top, right sides inside, and tack through three thicknesses. Stitch. Take out tacking stitches, turn to right side and press (Fig 47b). Place collar inside blouse and stitch one edge of collar to neck edge of blouse, beginning and finishing at hem line. Hem the other edge of collar to neck line. Press. Fasten the front with three press studs, beginning at centre top. Fasten left side over right. Finish each cuff with a press stud, fastening the front edge over back.

Fig 47

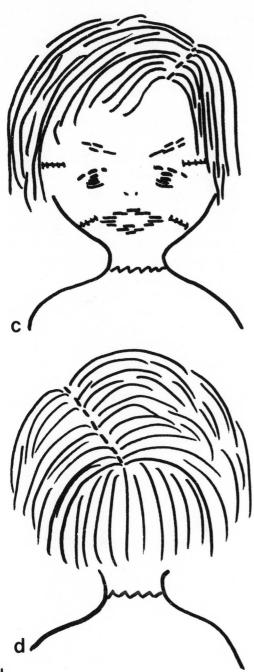

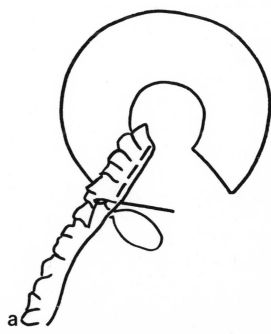

Head
The front and back are both the same. On one piece place As together and oversew seam. Place Bs together and oversew seam. Continue all round in this way. Stitch seams in the other piece of head. Oversew the two head pieces together, matching As, Bs, Cs, Ds, Es and Fs. Turn to right side. Stuff firmly. Ladderstitch the neck of head on top of the neck edge of body, adding more stuffing as necessary to make a very firm neck.

Hair
Cut crochet cotton into 8 in (20·3 cm) lengths. Backstitch to head with double thread as shown in Figs 46a and b). Fold the right side hair over seams. Arrange

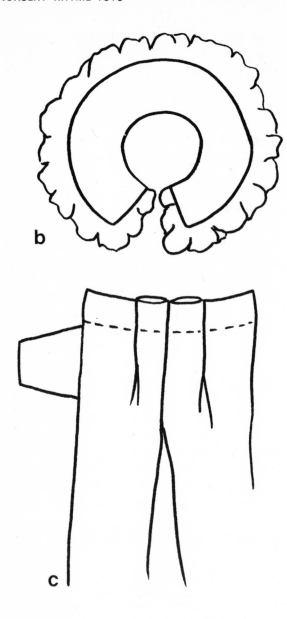

b

c

Jacket

Oversew shoulder, side and sleeve seams. Turn to right side. Fasten left front over right with three press studs. Stitch three buttons on top of stud on left side. Put on doll and bring the blouse collar over the top of jacket neckline.

Cap

Make this the same as for Pieman's hat. Then place the two pieces of peak together, right sides facing, and over-sew the curved edge. Turn to right side. Oversew one straight edge of peak to edge of cap band. Hem the other straight edge on top of seam. Wind black embroidery cotton five times over a piece of cardboard $1\frac{1}{4}$ in (3·2 cm) long. Thread a slim darning needle with a length of black embroidery thread. Tie strands of tassel together with end. Tear cardboard away. Pass needle down $\frac{1}{4}$ in (6 mm) inside tassel. Bring needle to outside and wind round four times. Fasten and push needle through inside, coming out at centre top. Push needle through centre top of cap. Leaving a 6 in (15·2 cm) length of thread, fasten off on the inside of cap with a large French knot. Put on doll slightly to one side at a jaunty angle.

Trousers

Stitch side seams from A to B and C to D. Press. Stitch from E to F. Stitch leg seams F to G. Press. Make a narrow hem on lower side leg from D to H. Press. Hem lower leg. Fold the pocket and stitch both sides. Turn and press. Stitch edge of pocket to edge of trouser between B and C, with pocket protruding on the out-side (Fig 47c). Make a hem at the top of trousers. Try on doll and fold the surplus material each side of centre front. Fasten folds with four press studs. This is an easy way to fasten trousers. Put on doll.

Socks

Stitch curved side. Hem top. Press and put on doll. Make another sock to match.

Shoes

Make as for pieman.

YANKEE DOODLE

Yankee Doodle went to town
Upon a little pony
He stuck a feather in his cap
And called it macaroni.

Fig 48

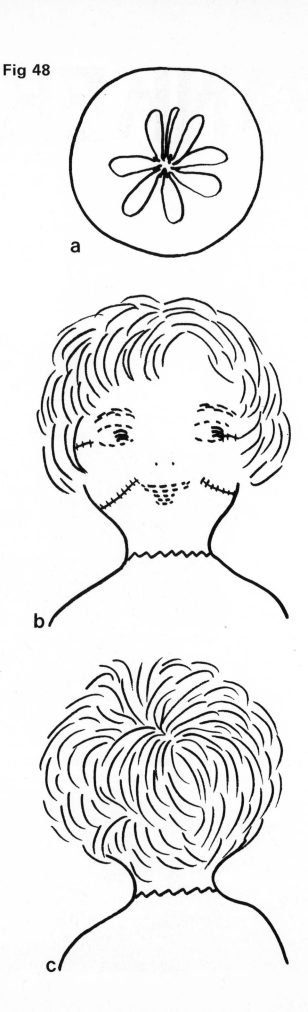

a

b

c

Patterns pp 134—149.

YANKEE DOODLE

Height 9 in (23 cm).

MATERIALS

Felt, flesh-coloured, 14½ in (37 cm) square for doll.
Small ball pale, honey-coloured crochet cotton for hair.
Embroidery cotton, red, white and brown.
Deep blue drill, 9 in × 11 in (23 cm × 28 cm) for trousers.
Strong cotton 15 in × 12½ in (38 cm × 32 cm) for blouse. The original used a blue, red and green stripe, which looks quite gay. Of course any bright colour may be used as a contrast to the trousers.
White stockinette, 6½ in × 3½ in (16·5 cm × 9 cm) for socks.
Eight press studs size 00.
Pipe cleaners.
Piece of wood, 5 in (12·7 cm) long, ¼ in (6 mm) diameter.
Light beige felt, 8¾ in × 9½ in (22·2 cm × 24 cm) for hat and boots.
Chamois leather, 4 in × 2½ in (10 cm × 6·4 cm) for boot soles.
Leather thonging, dark brown, 20 in (50·3 cm) for hat band.
Feather.
Hair lacquer.
Stuffing. Adhesive tape.

CUT

Head, body, legs, arms and hands the same as for Simple Simon in flesh-coloured felt.
Four boot soles, four boot uppers, two socks and two trouser pieces in materials described above.

Two blouse fronts, one blouse back, one collar, two cuffs and a 6 in (15·2 cm) circle for hat, all as listed above.

MAKING UP

Stitch doll exactly the same as for Simple Simon as far as hair.

Hair

Fasten crochet cotton to centre of head. Make a loop 2 in (5 cm) long and fasten. Continue making loops until a circle of loops has been made (Fig 48a). Now make another circle of loops ½ in (1·3 cm) from first circle. Continue to cover the head in this way. Now cut the loops at the end. Trim the hair (Fig 48b and c).

Features

Consulting Fig 48b and using one strand of embroidery cotton, embroider eyes in white and brown. Embroider mouth and nose in red. Eyelashes and eyebrows in brown.

Trousers

Stitch back seam and front seam from A to B. Stitch inner leg seams. Press. Make a dart ¾ in (2 cm) each side of back seam. Make a similar dart each side of front opening, stitch a piece of binding on seamline each side of front opening (Fig 49a). Turn back the left-hand piece and hem to front (Fig 49b). Fold the right-hand piece to form an underlap and hem on seamline. Press. Make a narrow hem at top. Press. Close the front opening with two press studs (Fig 49c). Try on doll and adjust length of legs. Make a hem at lower edge of each leg.

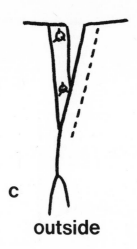

c outside

Fig 49

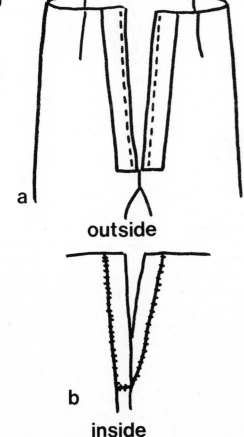

a

outside

b

inside

Socks

Stitch curved side. Hem top. Press. Put on doll. Make another sock to match.

Boots

Oversew two pieces of boot together from A to B, and C to D. Turn to right side. Make soles as for Pieman. Stabstitch the boot upper to sole on outside (Fig 50). Put on doll over trouser legs.

Fig 50

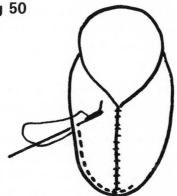

Blouse

Fold back of blouse in half, wrong sides together, and stitch for 2¼ in (5·7 cm) from top, ⅜ in (1 cm) in from fold (Fig 51a). Press pleat flat in centre (Fig 51b). Stitch shoulder and sleeve seams. Stitch underarm and side seams from A to D. Make a narrow hem at each front. Make collar as for Pieman and stitch to neck. Fold collar so that it lies neatly. Finish front with four press studs. Make and finish cuffs as for Simple Simon. Make a narrow hem on the side seam slits. Press. Make a narrow hem on lower edge. Press and put on doll.

Fig 51

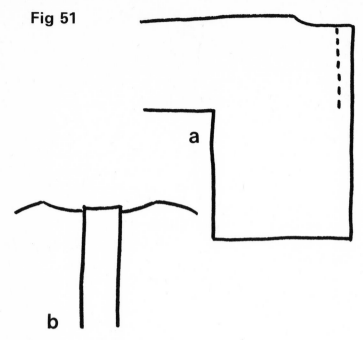

a

b

Hat

You will need a cup or a jar with a 2½ in (6·4 cm) diameter base for this. Turn upside down on a table or board, somewhere where it may be left for a while to dry. Lay the hat circle in water to get thoroughly soaked. Place over the centre of upturned cup. Model the crown by stroking from the centre, down the sides for ½ in (1·3 cm). If you gradually ease the water out in this way, you will find the hat will take shape.

Gently turn two sides upwards and over, towards crown, so that it looks like a cowboy's hat (Fig 52a). Leave to dry. Make a small slit close to crown in the centre of each side of hat. Stitch one end of leather thong on left side close to slit. Take thong round front, down through slit on right side, up through slit on left side and round back of hat to right side (Fig 52b). Stitch the end neatly. Push the end of feather through hat band on left side, and keep firm with a few neat stitches. Put on doll and knot thong under the chin (Fig 52c).

Fig 52

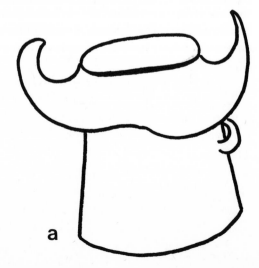

a

b

c

PONY

Height 14 in (35·6 cm).

MATERIALS

Felt, brown, 16 in × 36 in (40·6 cm × 91·4 cm).
Chamois leather, 3 in × 6 in (7·6 cm × 15·2 cm).
Hair, strands 9 in (23 cm) long. The original used hair obtained from a hairdresser, but wool or raffia may be used with equally good results.
Two wooden suit coat-hangers with bar.
Two brass rings, ½ in (1·3 cm) diameter.
Two 16 mm brown eyes.
Black leather strips ¼ in (6 mm) wide, 42 in (107 cm) long. ⅛ in (3 mm) wire: two pieces 21 in (53 cm), one piece 4 in (10 cm).

CUT

Pony's body in the following way: trace the front part of pony on brown felt; place the dotted lines to the dotted lines on back part of pony and continue to trace so that the whole of the pony will be in one piece. Make a cardboard template of this and two in brown felt to match.

Two inner back and front legs, one body gusset, one head gusset, two eyelids and two inner and outer ears, all in brown felt.

Four chamois hoofs and hoofbases and four cardboard hoof bases.

MAKING UP

Oversew inner front legs to body gusset from D to B. Stitch other side to match. Oversew inner back legs to body gusset from F to H. Stitch other side to match. Oversew gusset to body from B to F. Continue leg seam from F to E. Now oversew leg seam from B to A, from D to C and G to H. Stitch other side to match. Stitch from K to D both sides.

Head gusset

Oversew one side to head from Z to K. Starting at Z again, stitch other side to match. If you are using real hair, stick this along a piece of tape 7 in (17·8 cm) long for mane, and 2 in (5 cm) for tail. If you are using wool or raffia, this can be stitched to tape. Starting at Z, lay the mane tape along top of head and neck on right side. Place the other piece of head and neck on top so that the mane lies on right side. Now backstitch the mane, on wrong side, making sure the tape does not show on right side. Stuff the head and neck firmly.

Tail

Oversew the back from H to J. Roll the tail and lay at J. Stitch on inside.

Rockers

Shape one piece of wire to fit the two front legs (see dotted line on pattern), with $3\frac{1}{2}$ in (9 cm) joining them at the bottom. Bind with adhesive tape. Remove hooks from hangers, place hangers upside-down, side by side, and pass the leg wire between curved and straight bars of both. Push wire into front legs of pony and stuff round them firmly. Continue stuffing until chest is firm, gradually ladderstitching opening. Shape the other piece of wire to fit back legs and bind with tape. Place through bars of the two hangers as for front legs, and push into back legs of pony. Stuff round wire firmly. Continue stuffing back, ladderstitching opening

gradually. Be sure to stuff firmly and keep a good shape. Cover the pieces of wire between the legs with a strip of brown felt. Oversew back seam of chamois leather hoof. Oversew hoof to base. Turn to right side. Place the cardboard base inside and stuff firmly. Put over end of leg with seam at back. Hem to leg, putting in small pieces of stuffing as necessary to make a very firm finish (Fig 53a). Hem a piece of brown felt to the inside of leg, just above hoof (Fig 53b). Fold the ends over the wooden bar and hem firmly (Fig 53c). This will keep the pony firmly attached to the rockers. Finish the other legs in the same way. Bend the ends of the 4 in (10 cm) piece of wire to fit in the two holes in the centre of the hangers. Cover with a strip of brown felt and fix in place.

Fig 53

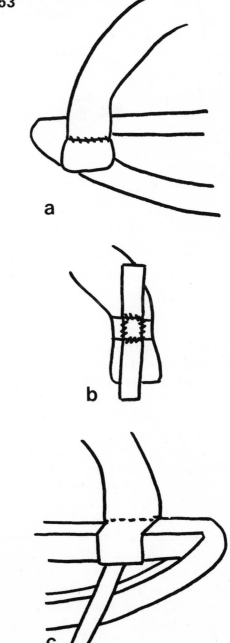

a

b

c

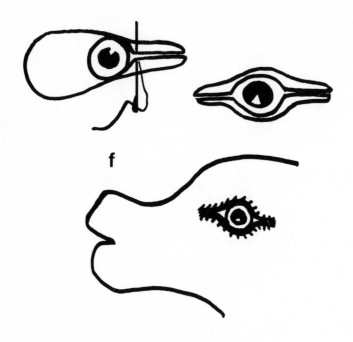

f

Divide the end of the mane and bring over front of head. Dampen to keep in place and, when dry, trim neatly.

Reins

Cut lengths of leather 3 in (7·6 cm), 4 in (10·2 cm), 7½ in (19 cm) and 4½ in (11·4 cm). Stitch as shown in Fig 54c. Put on pony.

Sit Yankee Doodle on pony's back, bending legs as required to grip. Arrange reins in hands, and bend fingers over to hold.

Fig 54

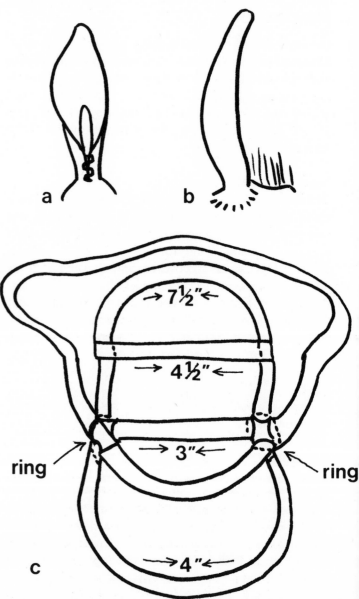

Eyes

Push the eye wire through the centre of brown felt eyelid circle (Fig 53d). Turn the end of wire back on itself and twist to neaten (Fig 53e). Thread long thin needle through eye position in pony. Bring out at the eye position on opposite side of face. Fasten firmly. Insert the other eye in the same way. Fold the felt over eye to form upper and lower lids. Stabstitch both sides of eyelid so that the eye fits snugly and firmly in the socket (Fig 53f). Ladderstitch outer edge to head.

Ears

Place two pieces together and oversew all round except straight edge. Turn to right side. Fold in half and ladderstitch the two sides together for ½ in (1·3 cm) at the bottom, as shown in Fig 54a. With the end spread open, ladderstitch ear to head at gusset seam (Fig 54b). Finish other ear to match.

JACK AND JILL

**Jack and Jill went up the hill
To fetch a pail of water ;
Jack fell down and broke his crown,
And Jill came tumbling after.**

Patterns pp 150–159.

JACK & JILL

Height 17 in (43 cm).

MATERIALS

Dolls

(The materials listed are for one doll only, but both are made in exactly the same way. Both dolls are jointed.)
Felt, flesh-coloured, 18 in × 20 in (45·7 cm × 50 cm) for body, one piece large enough to cover a 4 in (10·2 cm) face well and a few extra scraps.
Metal joint sets, two 1¼ in (3·2 cm), two 1 in (2·5 cm) and one 1½ in (3·8 cm).
Stuffing.
Pipe cleaners.
Cardboard.
Embroidery cotton, blue, red, white and brown, for features.
½ oz honey-coloured soft double knitting wool for hair.
4 in (10·2 cm) face mould (this can be an old doll's head, a wooden carving, or one could be fashioned in Plasticine).
Small piece of lawn and some thin paper.
Cold cream.
Paste (paperhanger's paste or flour-and-water will do).

Jack's outfit

¾ oz 2-ply white wool, one pair of knitting needles (size 12) and one set of four double-ended needles (size 14) for vest and socks.

Blue cotton material, 20 in × 15 in (50·8 cm × 38 cm) for suit (original was made from oddments of blue denim, with the white selvedge used to make an edging).
Strong navy linen or felt and small piece of chamois leather for shoes.
Tape for shoe laces.
Five small press studs.
Small piece of elastic.
Copydex.

Jill's outfit

Vest, socks and shoes as for Jack.
Fine white lawn, 18 in × 36 in (45·7 cm × 91·4 cm) for petticoat and pants.
Cotton with ⅜ in (1 cm) check, 18 in × 36 in (45·7 cm × 91·4 cm) for dress.
Embroidery cotton for smocking, to match or contrast dress material.
Bias binding to match dress material.
Narrow lace, 108 in (2·74 m).
Seven press studs.
Small piece of narrow elastic.

Pail

Grey felt, 9 in × 4 in (23 cm × 10·2 cm).
Cardboard, 7½ in × 3 in (19 cm × 7·6 cm).
Adhesive tape.
Grey sewing thread.

CUT

Two body pieces, two pairs of legs, two pairs of arms, two soles for feet, two pairs of hand pieces and two head backs, all in flesh-coloured felt.

All outfit pieces according to pattern and in materials listed above.

MAKING UP

Mask

It is rather fun to make an individual face-mask to suit the particular character, but if you do not feel you want to cope with making the moulded face, masks may be purchased ready to stitch on. The one in the photograph was made as follows :

1. First cover the mould with cold cream.
2. Soak the lawn in the paste, wring out and cover the face completely, fitting well into the corners of eyes and mouth.
3. Soak paper in the same way and place on top of lawn, again paying attention to corners of eyes and mouth.
4. Soak flesh-coloured felt well and cover face in same way as before.
5. Leave for two or three days in a warm, dry place. The mould should then be thoroughly dry and can be eased off gently.

Fig 55

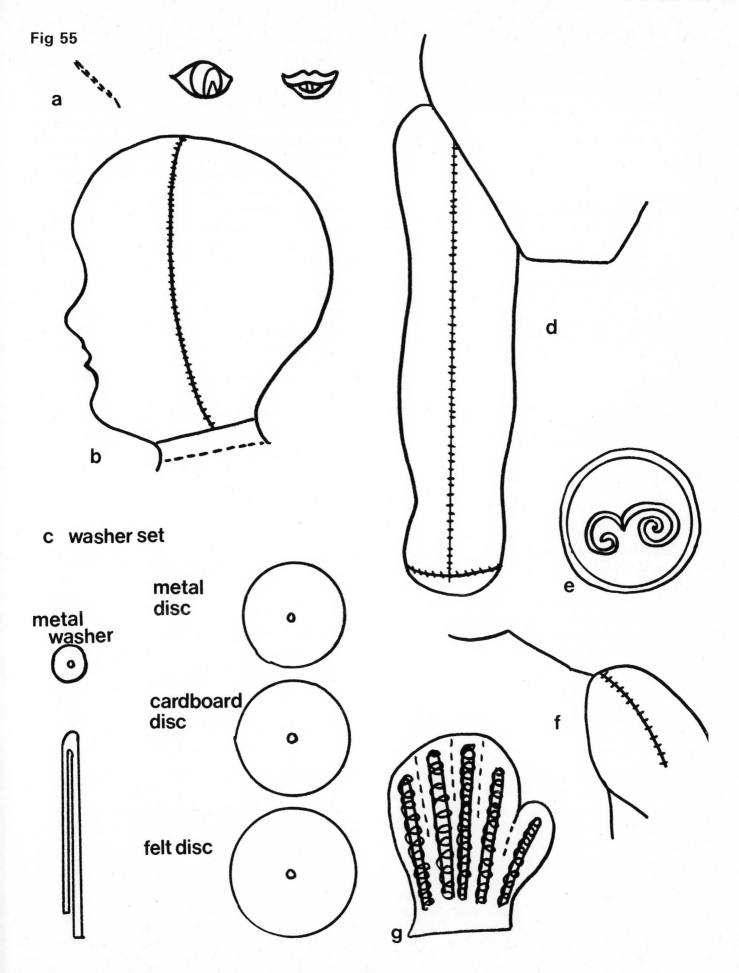

a

b

c washer set

metal
disc

metal
washer

cardboard
disc

felt disc

d

e

f

g

Jack's features

Using single thread, embroider the whole of the eye socket in white satin stitch. Then embroider a brown iris and finally a white highlight on top of that. Next embroider eyebrows in brown backstitch. Work the lips in red satin stitch following the shape of model, and finally work two small spots underneath the nose (Fig 55a).

Jill's features

Work exactly as for Jack, but use blue embroidery thread for iris instead of brown.

Head

Stitch back seam of two head pieces, leaving A to B open. Oversew back of head to face, on wrong side. Run a thread all round the lower edge, pull up and fasten (Fig 55b). Put aside while body is assembled.

Body

Take two leg pieces and oversew from A to C and B to D with small stitches. Match the D on leg to D on sole, and oversew all the way round. Turn right side out. Stuff firmly. Make other leg to match, making sure one is right and one left.

Stitch the arm pieces from A to C and from B to D. Turn right side out. Gather lower edge CD. Fasten off securely. Stuff firmly. Stitch the two body pieces together all round, except the top from A to B, and from C to D. Turn right side out. Gather neck and fasten off. Now joint the legs. Take one $1\frac{1}{4}$ in (3·2 cm) joint set, which consists of two metal discs, two cardboard discs, one cotter pin and one small metal washer. Cut two felt discs a little larger than cardboard disc (Fig 55c). Thread one metal washer, metal disc, cardboard disc and felt disc on the cotter pin, in that order. Push the pin through the fabric of the leg where the leg will be joined to body (marked X on pattern). Finish stuffing leg and ladderstitch top to close. The washer should rest directly against the inside of the leg material at the top, but the sides should be stuffed very firmly so that you will not be able to feel the washer at all once the leg is attached to the body. Repeat the process for the other leg, making sure that they are a pair (i.e. that the joints are fixed to the inner sides of the legs, and that the legs are both the same height). Now take the right leg and push the cotter pin through the slanting seam on body (Fig 55d). Put the other felt disc, cardboard disc and metal disc on cotter pin. Take a pair of pliers with a small nose and grip the edge of one prong of the cotter pin firmly, and turn under. Turn under and under until the washer is quite firm. Do the same with

the other prong of cotter pin (Fig 55e). Fix the arms in the same way, using the 1 in (2·54 cm) joints (Fig 55f). Take the head and fit the $1\frac{1}{4}$ in (3·8 cm) joint set through the centre of the lower edge.

Stuff the head very firmly, paying careful attention to the indentations of eyes, nose, etc. When it is very firmly stuffed, ladderstitch the back of head, pushing in just that little extra stuffing as you go. Now push the ends of cotter pin through the gathered neck edge of body and finish off firmly. Stuff the body using small pieces to avoid lumpiness, making sure it is quite firm over the joints, or the doll will be floppy and wobbly. Ladderstitch C to D gradually.

Hands

Take one pair of hands and oversew all round outside edge from C to D. Turn right side out. Stitch between fingers and thumb as indicated on pattern. Push a piece of double pipe cleaner into each finger and thumb (Fig 55g). Put a little stuffing over ends of pipe cleaner to make a palm, and a very little at back of hand and wrist. With the thumb uppermost, hem the hand to arm, using small stitches. The fingers may now be bent to hold the pail. Finish the other hand and hem to arm in the same way.

Fig 56

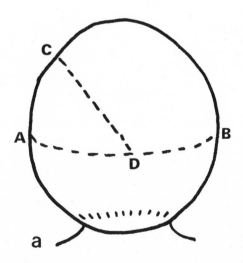

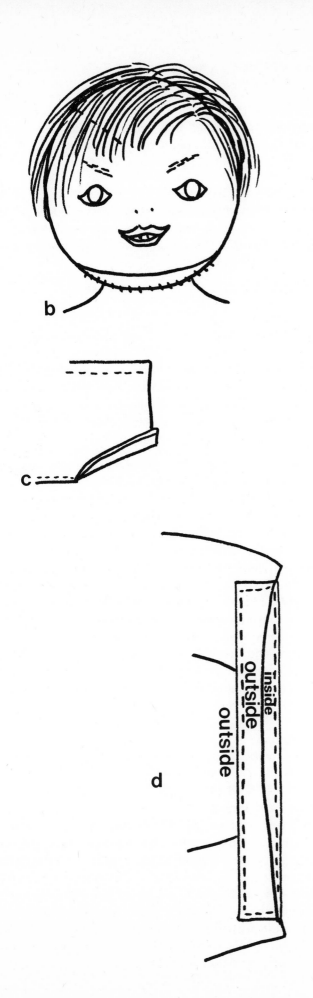

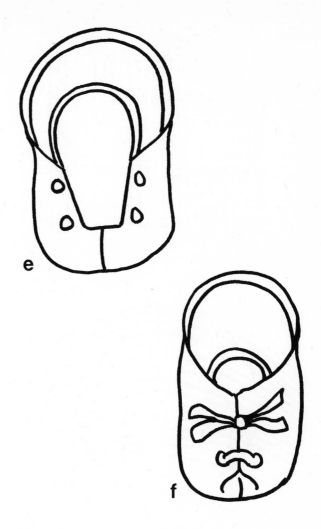

Jack's hair

Cut wool in bundles 10 in (25·4 cm) long. Lay very thickly on head, with the ends coming 1 in (2·5 cm) up from neck, and stitch all round from A to B (Fig 56a). Make another row of stitching from C to D. Take a few of the strands above C–D line and turn them back over the stitching line. Draw the rest across the head in a forward line. Stitch the bottom layer to head to keep position and brush the rest forward. Trim all round to a neat small-boyish look (Fig 56b).

Jill's hair

Take a bundle of honey-coloured wool 6 in (15 cm) long and lay lengthwise from front to back of head in order to make a fringe. Backstitch just beyond seamline on top of head (Fig 57a). Cut bundles of wool and lay across head over fringe, down the back, to within 1 in (2·5 cm) from base of neck (Fig 57b). Backstitch the wool to head starting from centre front of fringe. Trim the fringe. Divide the hair in half and make a small plait each side. Finish with two bows. Trim the ends and brush out a little so that the plaits stand out each side (Fig 57c).

Fig 57

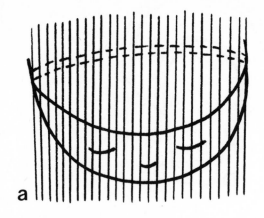

a

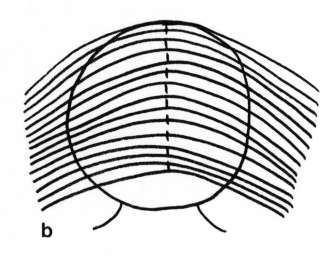

b

c

Jack's outfit

1. Vest

Using white 2-ply wool and No 12 needles, cast on 48 sts. K2 P2 rib for 3 in (7·6 cm).
Cast off 8 sts at start of next two rows. Continue on

these 32 sts for a further 2¼ in (5·7 cm). Cast off. Knit another piece exactly the same.

Press each piece under a damp cloth very lightly. Oversew the side seams. Sew press studs to each end of neck edge, the front overlapping the back.

2. Pants

Join front and back seams from A to B. Stitch inner leg seams. If you have used material with a selvedge, you may turn up a cuff, slanting gradually from inner leg to ½ in (1·3 cm) at the sides. If there is no selvedge, bind edge and turn up.

Hem round top of pants and insert elastic.

3. Jacket

Join raglan sleeves to front and back pieces of jacket. Starting ½ in (3 cm) in from sleeve edge, stitch sleeve and side seams. Turn to right side and stitch the remaining ½ in (3 cm) on sleeve. Turn this back to form cuff. If preferred, the edge may be bound, or, if it is a selvedge, may be left altogether. Make a ¾ in (2 cm) hem on each front edge of jacket.

Make a narrow turning on one long edge and two short edges of both collar pieces. Tack them together, right sides outside, and stitch with contrasting colour cotton. Lay the collar on the outside of jacket neck edge. Tack and stitch two thicknesses only, leaving ¼ in (6 mm) each end of jacket free (Fig 56d). Turn jacket inside out and hem the loose collar piece over the seam just made. Turn in the ends and oversew with small stitches. Make a narrow hem at lower edge of jacket, or bind. Make a very narrow hem on pocket. Turn in and tack three sides. Pencil the word JACK on the pocket and work in backstitch with one thread of embroidery cotton. Hem the pocket in place on jacket. Sew three press studs 1½ in (4 cm) apart, the first one at the collar.

4. Socks

Using white 2-ply wool and set of 4 double-ended needles, cast on 48 stitches (16 on each needle).
Work six rounds K1 P1 rib.
Work 12 rounds K.
To divide for heel, put 24 stitches on the first needle and 12 on each of two other needles. Using the first 24 only, work 18 rows stocking stitch, slipping each first stitch.
Next row: K15, slip 1, K1, psso. Turn. P7, slip 1, P1, psso. Turn. K7, slip 1, K1, psso. Turn. Continue in this way until all stitches have been used and 8 stitches remain on needle. K4. Transfer all stitches from other two needles onto one needle. You now have 4 stitches on

first needle, 24 stitches on second needle and 4 stitches on third needle. Continue as follows.

K4 from heel needle, pick up and K8 stitches along side heel. Second needle K24. Third needle pick up and K8 stitches along side of heel, K4 from needle. K1 round. Next round: first needle K to the last 3 stitches, K2 tog through the back of stitches; second needle K; third needle K1, slip 1, K1, psso, K to the end of round.

Repeat these two rounds 3 times. K5 rounds.

Next round: K3, K2 tog. Repeat to end of round.

Next round: K.

Next round: K2, K2 tog. Repeat to end of round.

Next round: K.

Next round: K1, K2 tog. Repeat to end of round.

Next round: K.

Next round: K2 tog to end of round. Break wool and run thread through stitches on needles. Draw up and fasten off.

Make another sock in same way. Press. Put on doll.

5. Shoes

Take one pair of chamois leather soles and oversew the edges with small stitches, leaving X to X open. Turn to right side. Slip a cardboard sole in the opening and close neatly with ladderstitch. Stitch the shoe upper from A to B on wrong side. If using linen, make a narrow turning on lower edge B – B and stick with a little Copydex. While this is drying, make the other shoe to this point.

Place the seam on front of shoe to B on sole. Hem the upper to sole. Make a narrow turning at the top of shoe and glue in the same way. Make a narrow turning all round front and glue. When dry, punch four holes, two on each side of front, $\frac{1}{4}$ in (6 mm) from edge. Thread a piece of tape through holes for laces (Figs 56e and f).

Jill's outfit

1. Vest and socks
Exactly the same as for Jack.

2. Pants
Stitch side seams. Stitch leg seams. Hem round top for elastic. Make a very narrow hem round each leg and whip lace to the edge of each. Press. Thread elastic through waist. Put on doll.

3. Petticoat
Join side seams. Make a narrow hem all round armholes. Make a narrow hem along neck edges and each of the four shoulder pieces. Whip lace to all of these edges. Sew press stud on each shoulder, lapping front over back. Make a narrow hem round lower edge. Whip lace to hem.

4. Dress (Fig 58a)
To embroider front, start with right side of material facing, and at right armhole. Lap one full square over the next and tack. Continue in this way right along to the other armhole. Go back to the right armhole and repeat the tacking on the square underneath. Repeat again on the next row of squares. Using one strand of embroidery cotton, bring needle up at top right-hand corner on pleat. Make a small stitch in the same place and bring needle up in place 3. Continue in this way to the end. Starting at right-hand side again, bring needle up at A. Make a stitch, bring needle up at B and so on. When you have finished stitch D, bring the needle up again at 5 on the top row, and then down to E, and continue in this manner to the end of the row (Fig 58b). Cut the back of dress down the centre. Leaving $\frac{3}{4}$ in (2 cm) each side of centre back, embroider the two pieces to match the front.

Run a gathering thread $\frac{1}{4}$ in (6 mm) from lower edge of sleeves (Fig 58c). Pull up gathers to fit round top of arm and fasten thread. With right sides together, stitch a bias binding strip to lower edge (Fig 58d). Join sleeve to dress back and front (Fig 58e). Join shoulder seams of yoke (Fig 58f). With right sides facing, pin dress to yoke. Stitch (Fig 58g). Turn in and hem $\frac{1}{4}$ in (6 mm) on each side of centre back. With right sides facing, join a bias binding strip to neck edge. Turn in ends. Turn bias over edge and hem to seam. Stitch side seam and sleeve seam including bias binding. Turn bias binding on sleeve, and hem to seam. Trim the neck edge, ends of sleeves and the yoke seam with lace (Fig 59a). Make $\frac{1}{4}$ in (6 mm) hem at the bottom. Fasten the back with five press studs, one at the top and one at the bottom of the yoke, and the other three spaced equally down the skirt.

5. Shoes
Make a pair of soles as for Jack in chamois leather and cardboard. Turn under $\frac{1}{4}$ in (6 mm) on bottom of front shoe piece, and stick with a little Copydex. When this is dry, hem to sole between A and C (Fig 59b). Turn under $\frac{1}{4}$ in (6 mm) on one long end of shoe upper and glue. When dry, fold in half and put the centre of the fold to the centre of the heel and hem first one side to A, and then the other side to C (Fig 59b). Turn short side F – F under $\frac{1}{2}$ in (1·3 cm) and hem to side of front. Finish other side of front in same way. Turn under $\frac{1}{4}$ in (6 mm) all round top edge and glue. Fold the strap in half lengthways and stick. Try on doll and position strap to fit snugly across front of foot. Stitch strap to inside and fasten on outside with press stud (Fig 59c). Make another shoe in the same way, but make sure to fasten on the outside.

Fig 58

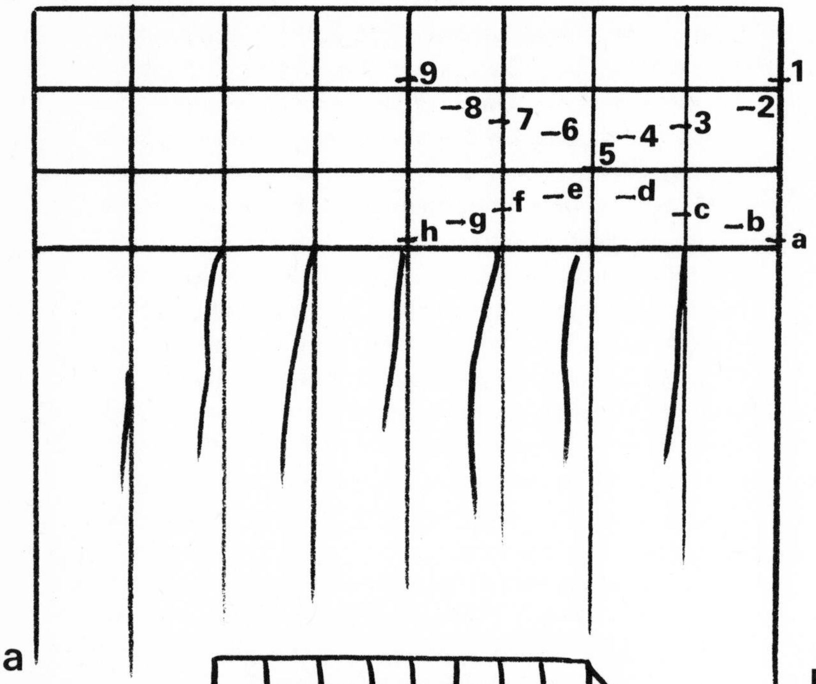

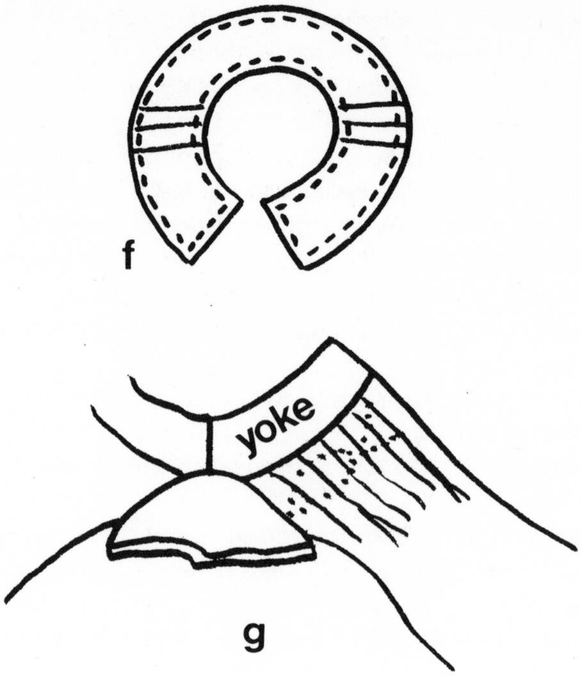

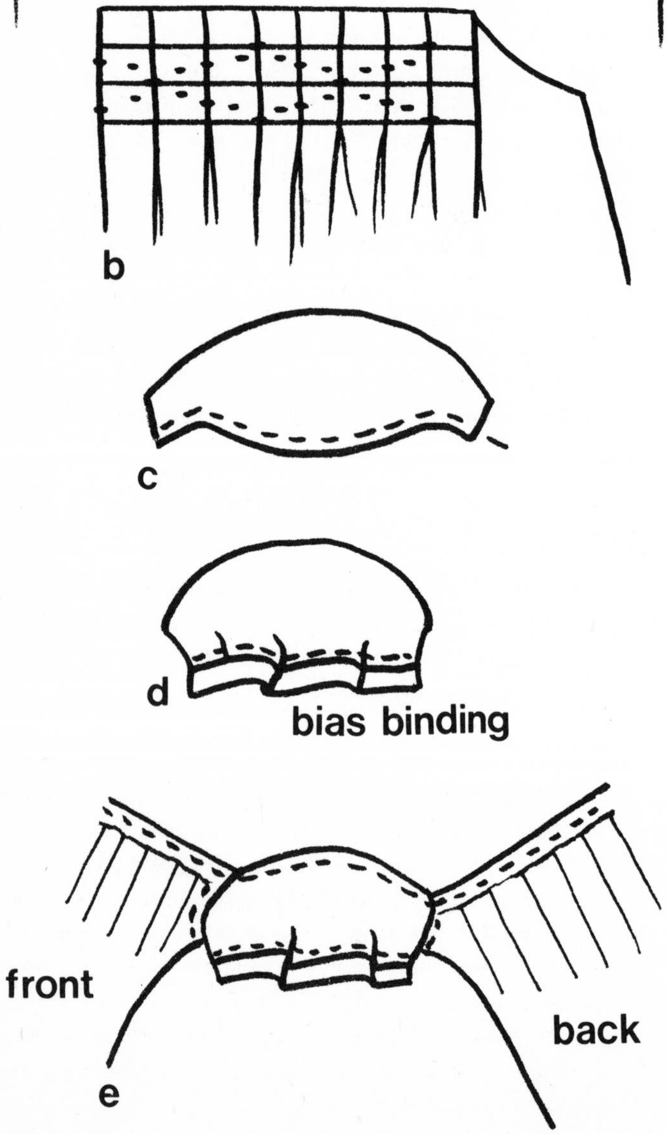

a

b

c

d

bias binding

front

back

e

f

yoke

g

Pail

Cut two pieces of adhesive tape $3\frac{1}{4}$ in (8·3 cm) long. Lay on a flat surface, sticky side up. Place the two pieces of cardboard A to A and B to B close together on top of the adhesive tape, leaving a small end of the tape to overlap at top and bottom (Fig 60a). Turn the ends of the tape over and press firmly. Take another piece of adhesive tape the same length. Lay on a flat surface and place one edge of pail along the centre (Fig 60b). Bend the other side carefully and place on the tape to match. Fold ends of tape over at top and bottom. Put aside. With small stitches, oversew both sides of grey felt pail. Stabstitch the base in place on the outside. Slip the cardboard inside. Fold the handle lengthways and stabstitch all the way round. Turn one end under, place $\frac{1}{2}$ in (1·3 cm) onto side seam of pail and stabstitch all round (Fig 60c). Finish other side to match.

Fig 59

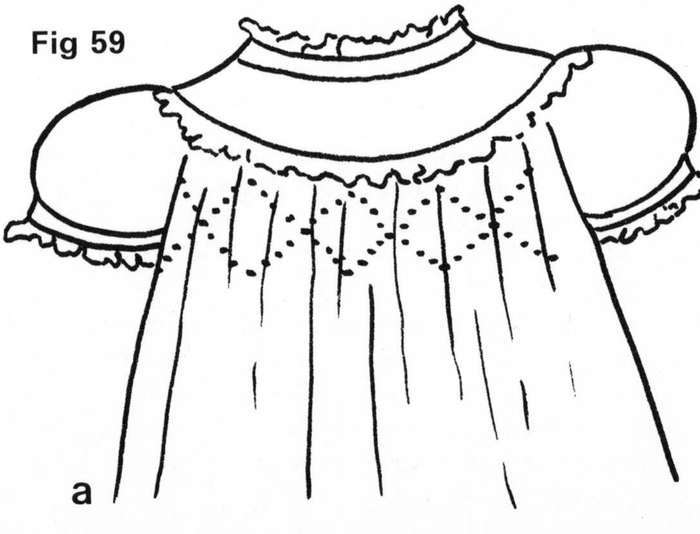

a

Fig 60

adhesive tape

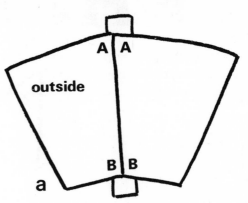

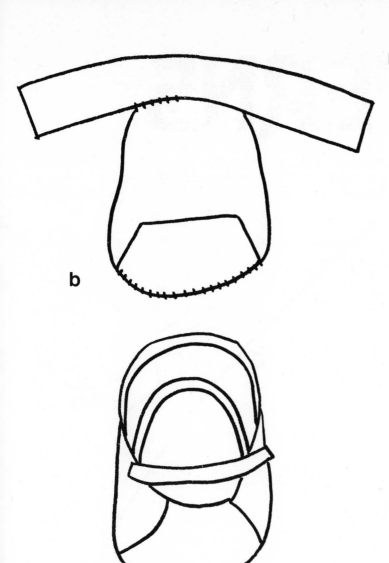

outside

A A

B B

a

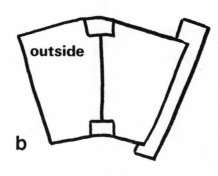

outside

b

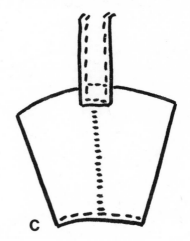

c

b

c

PATTERNS

HEY DIDDLE DIDDLE: Moon and Cow

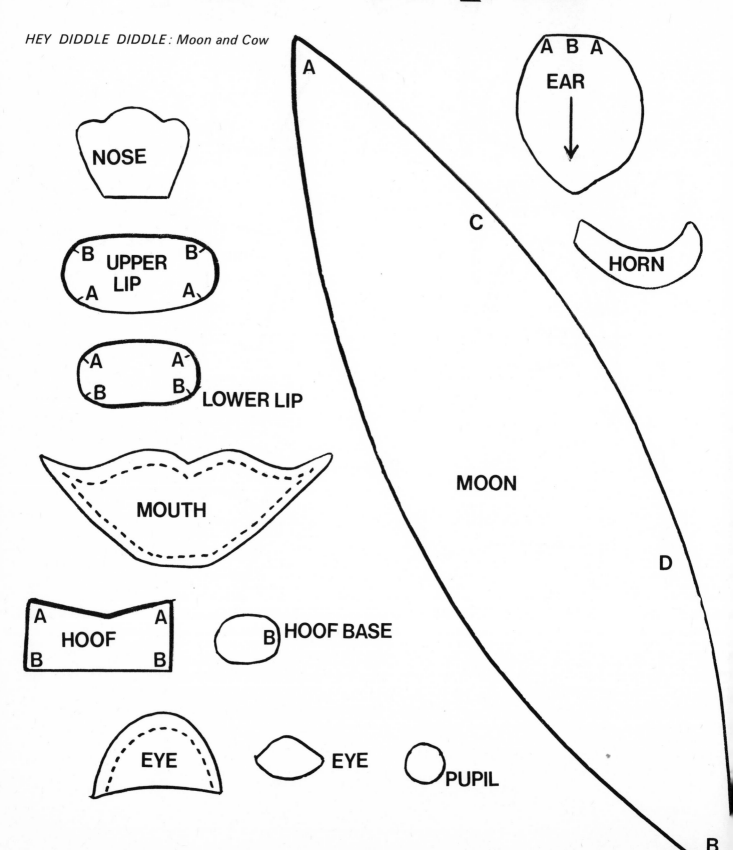

NOSE

B UPPER B
LIP
A   A

A   A
B   B   LOWER LIP

MOUTH

A   A
HOOF
B   B

B HOOF BASE

EYE

EYE

PUPIL

A B A
EAR

HORN

MOON

A

C

D

B

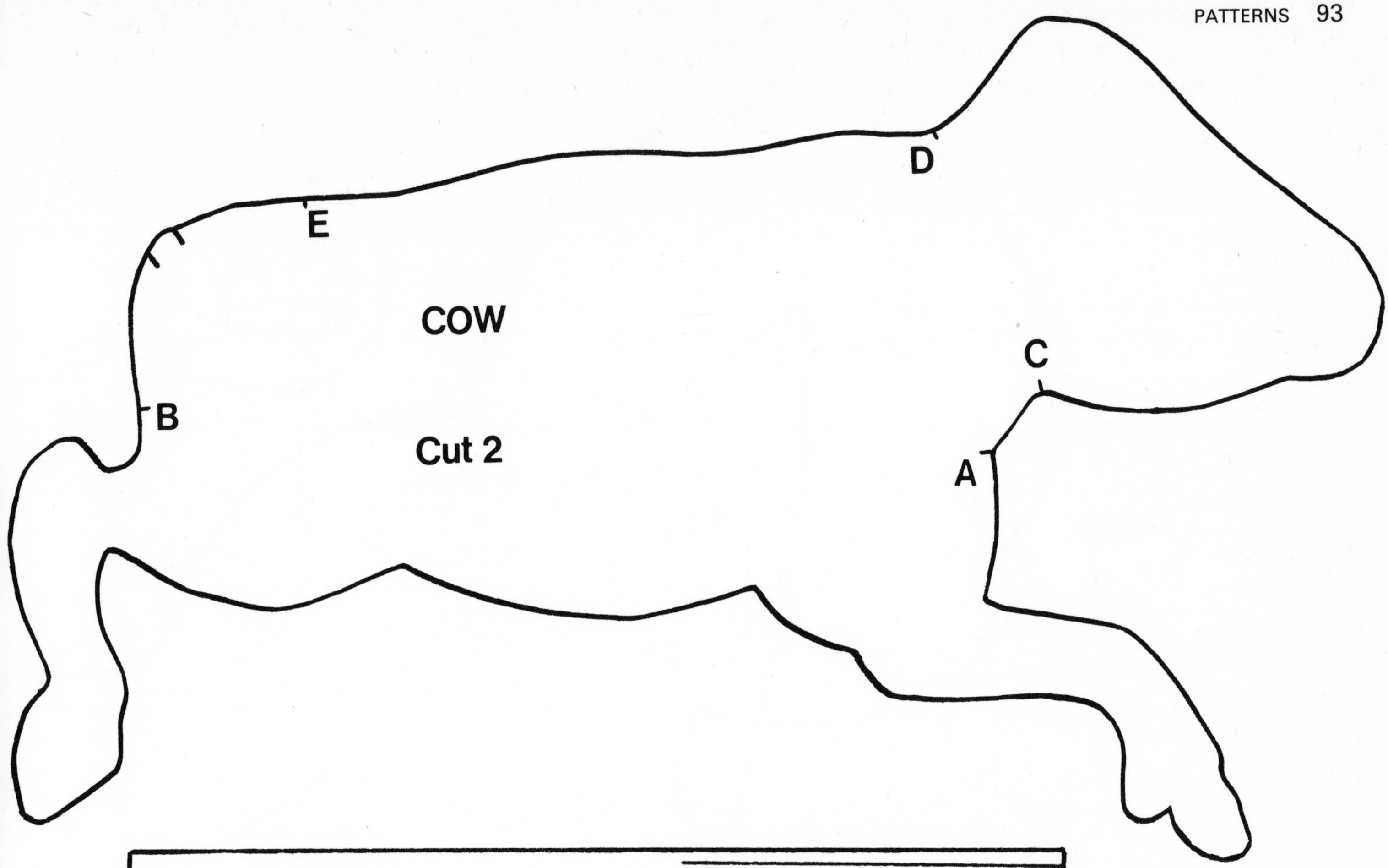

COW

Cut 2

E

D

B

C

A

TAIL

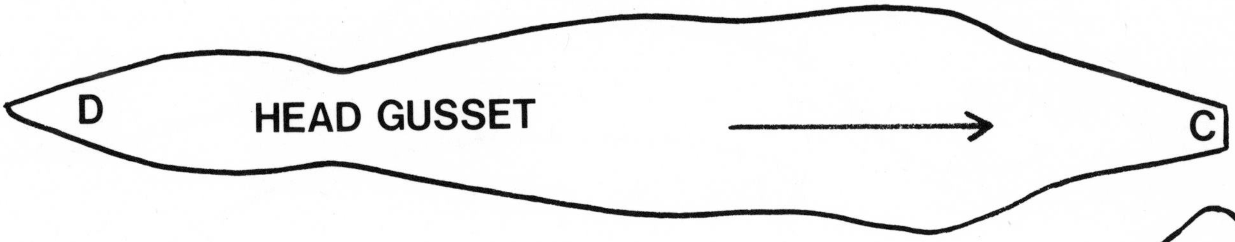

D HEAD GUSSET → C

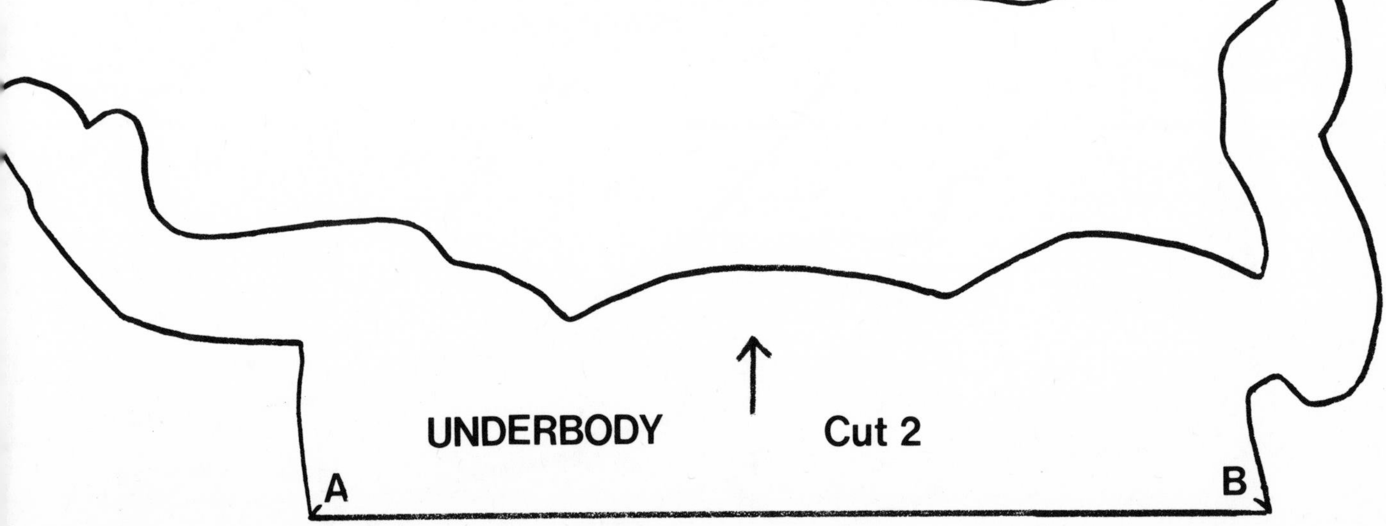

UNDERBODY ↑ Cut 2

A B

HEY DIDDLE DIDDLE: Cat and Fiddle

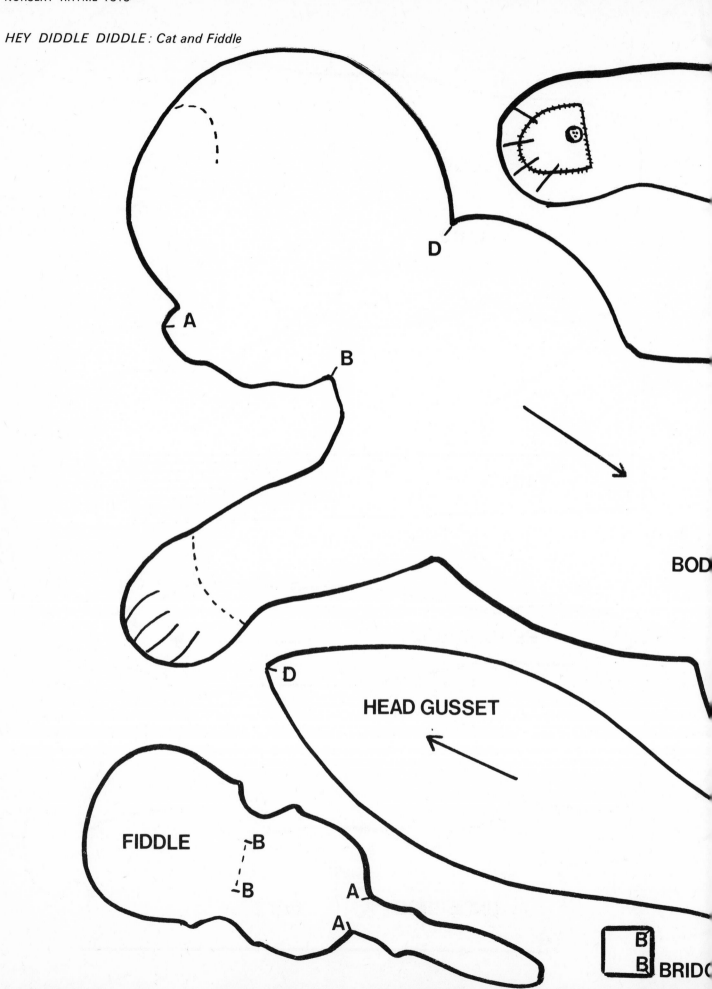

D

A

B

D

HEAD GUSSET

BOD

FIDDLE

B

B

A

A

B
B BRID

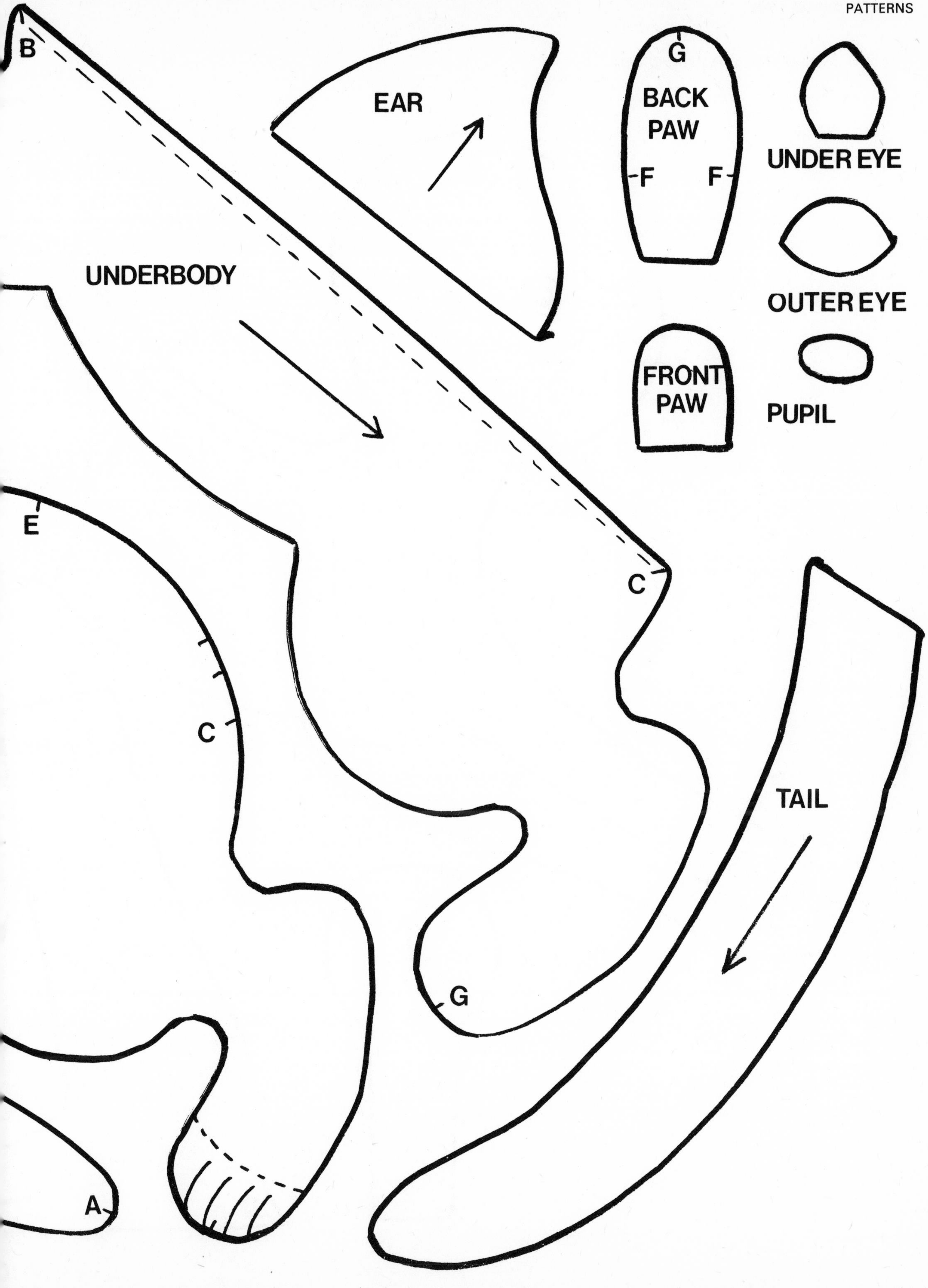

B

EAR

G

BACK
PAW

F   F

UNDER EYE

OUTER EYE

FRONT
PAW

PUPIL

UNDERBODY

E

C

C

TAIL

G

A

HEY DIDDLE DIDDLE: Laughing Dog

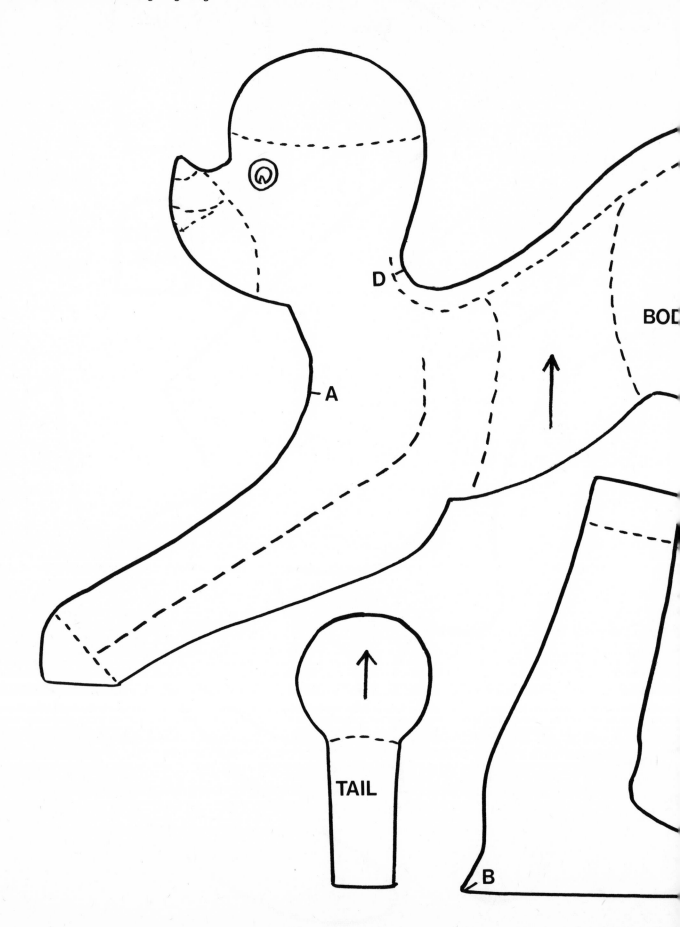

A

D

BOD

TAIL

B

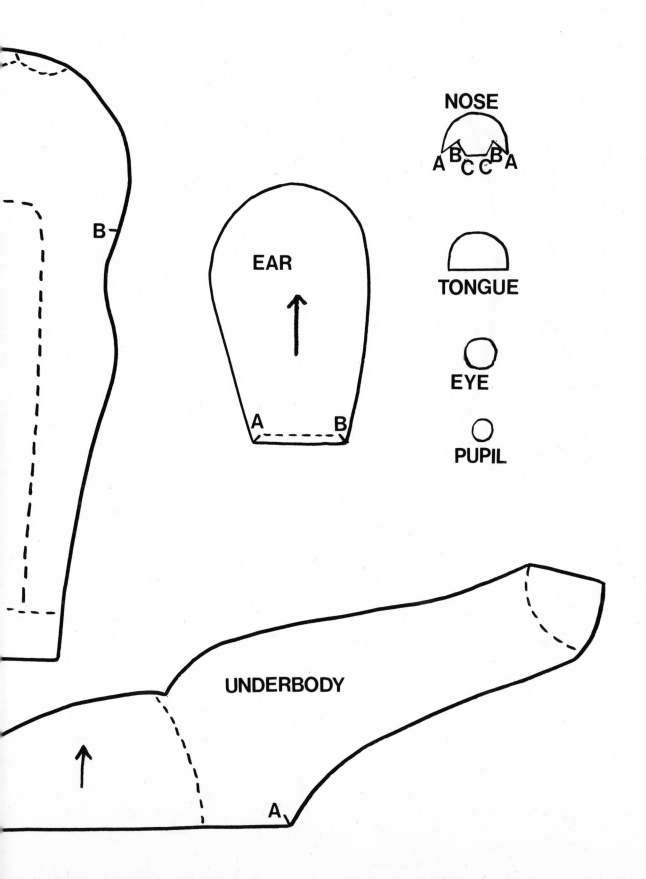

NOSE

A B C C B A

EAR

A B

TONGUE

EYE

PUPIL

UNDERBODY

A

B

HEY DIDDLE DIDDLE: Dish

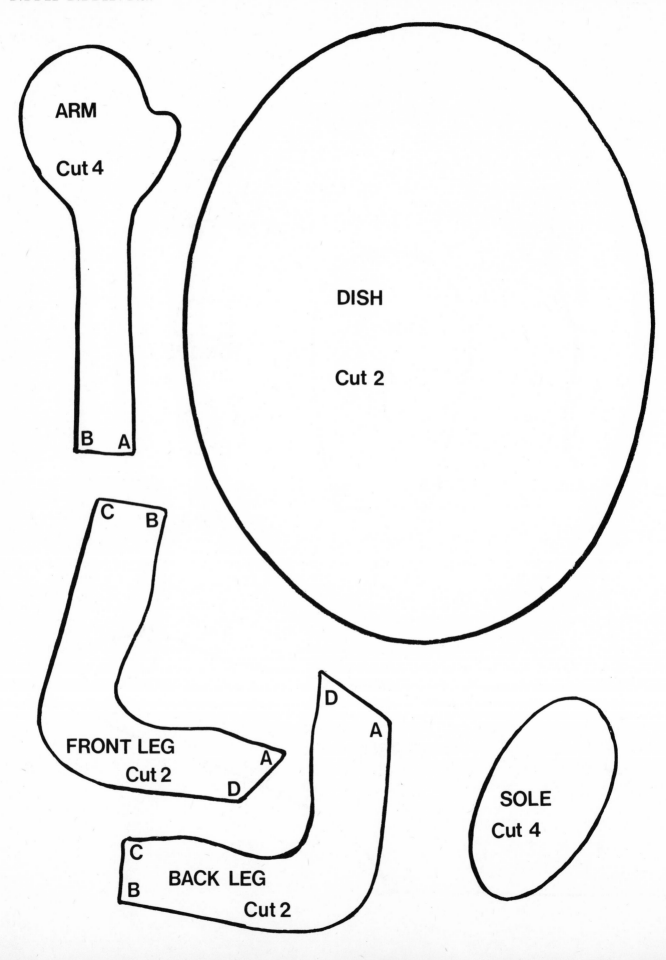

ARM

Cut 4

B   A

DISH

Cut 2

C   B

FRONT LEG

Cut 2

A

D

D

A

C

BACK LEG

B

Cut 2

SOLE

Cut 4

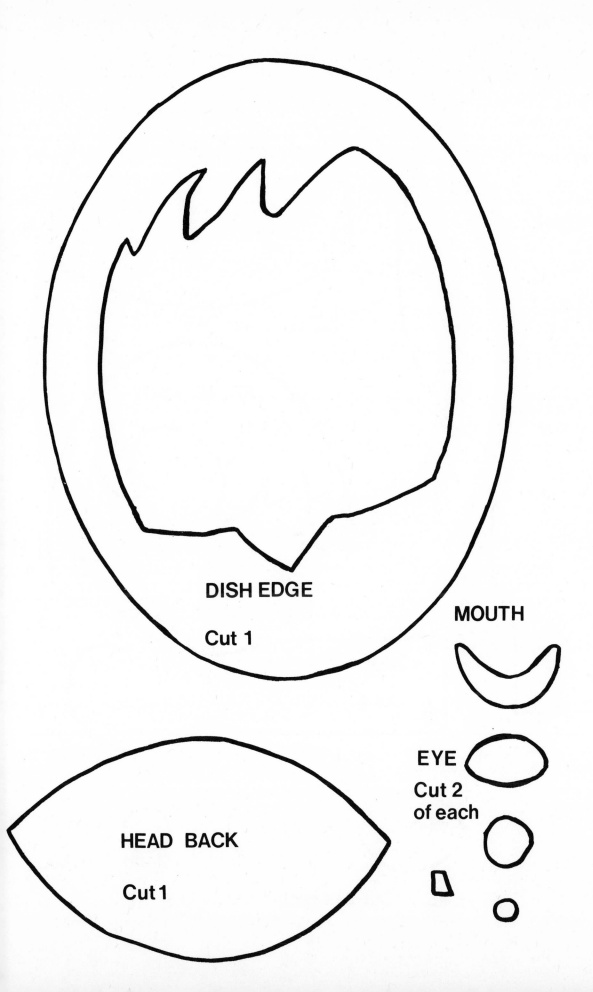

DISH EDGE

Cut 1

MOUTH

HEAD BACK

Cut 1

EYE

Cut 2
of each

HEY DIDDLE DIDDLE: Spoon

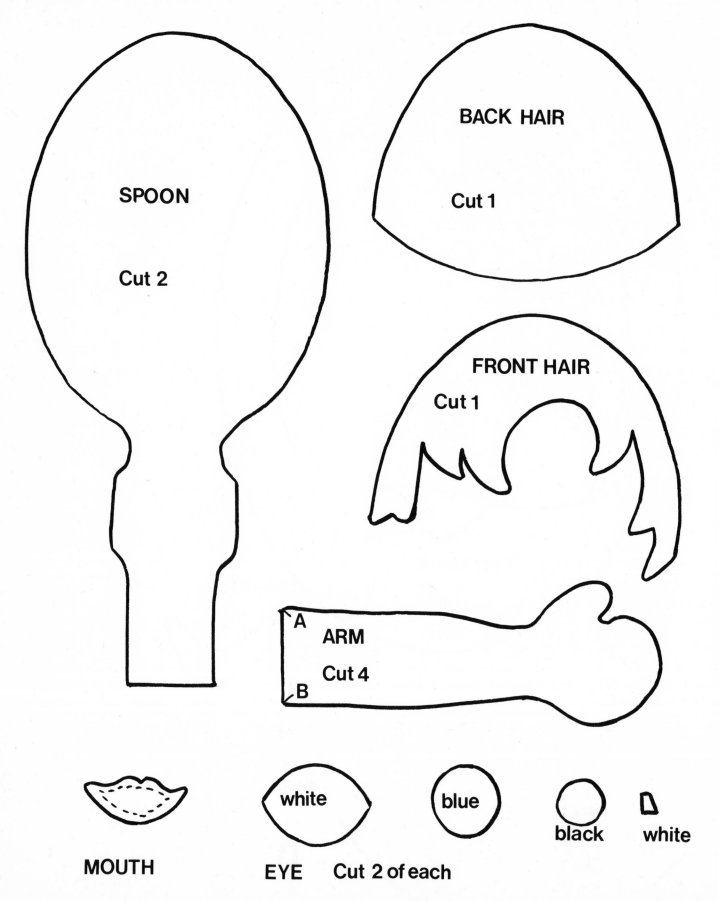

SPOON

Cut 2

BACK HAIR

Cut 1

FRONT HAIR

Cut 1

A

ARM

Cut 4

B

MOUTH

EYE   Cut 2 of each

white

blue

black

white

LITTLE BO-PEEP
LITTLE MISS MUFFET
LITTLE POLLY FLINDERS
POLLY PUT THE KETTLE ON

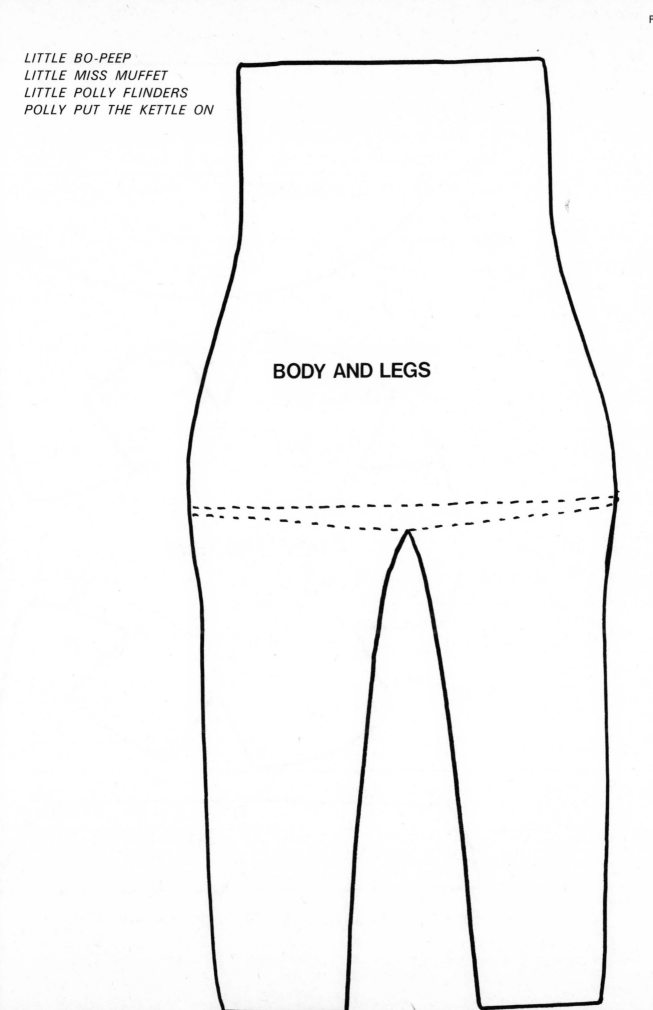

BODY AND LEGS

Polly Flinders

SLEEVE

E   E

D   E

D   D   F

F

F

Bo-Peep   Mi

Po

Po

HEAD AND ARMS

A

A

C   C   A

B

C   A

C   B   B

A   D   A

SHOE UPPER

D

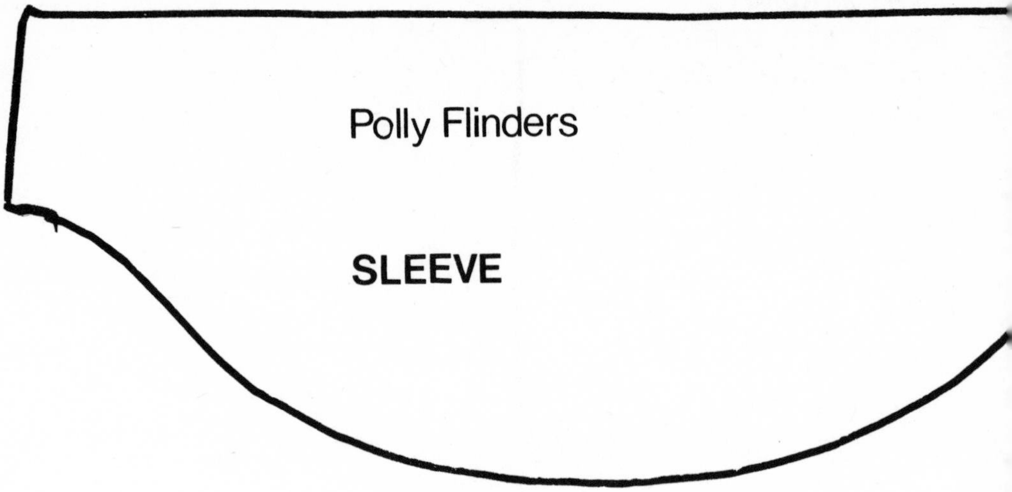

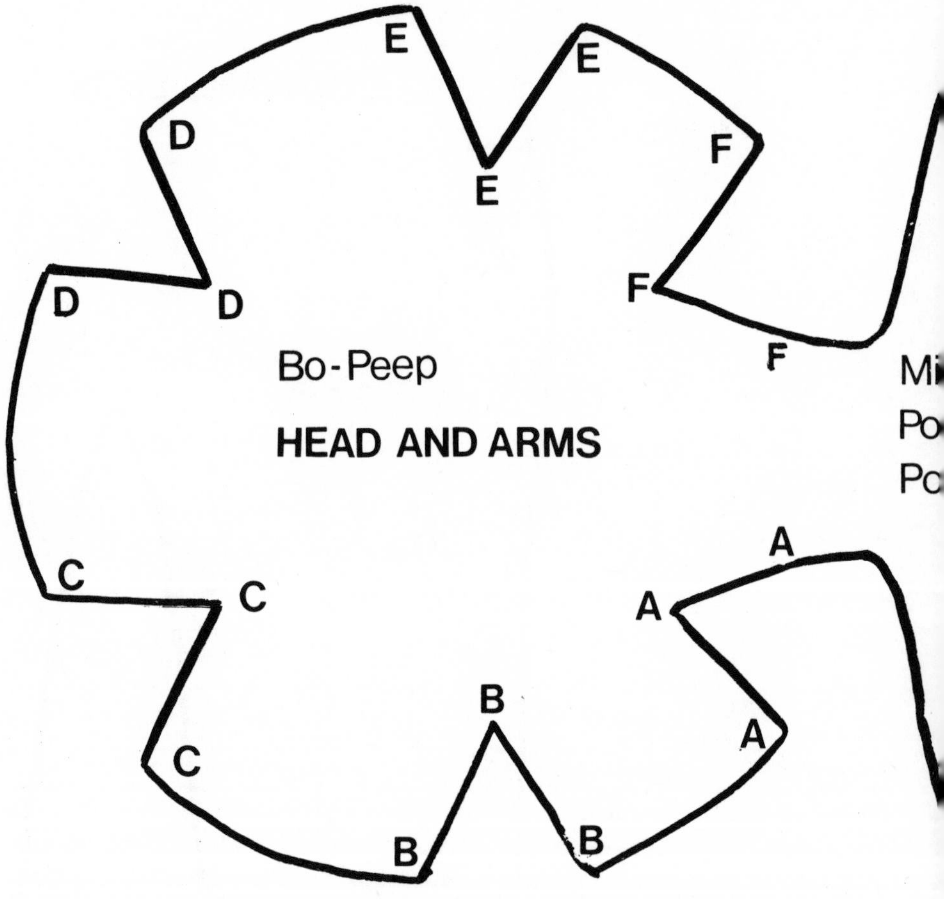

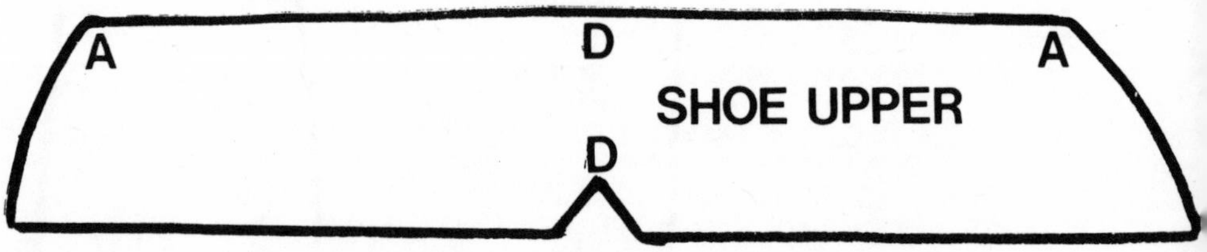

Bo-Peep   Miss Muffet   Polly put the kettle on

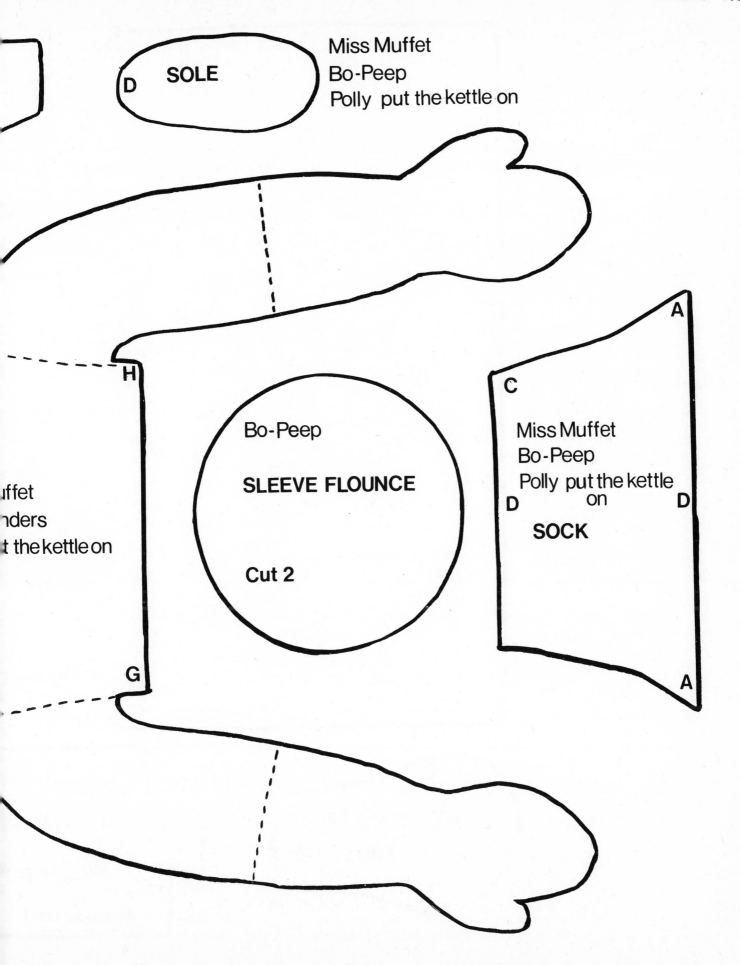

SOLE   D

Miss Muffet
Bo-Peep
Polly put the kettle on

H

Bo-Peep

SLEEVE FLOUNCE

Cut 2

uffet
nders
t the kettle on

G

A

C

Miss Muffet
Bo-Peep
Polly put the kettle
on   D

D

SOCK

A

LITTLE BO-PEEP
LITTLE MISS MUFFET
LITTLE POLLY FLINDERS
POLLY PUT THE KETTLE ON

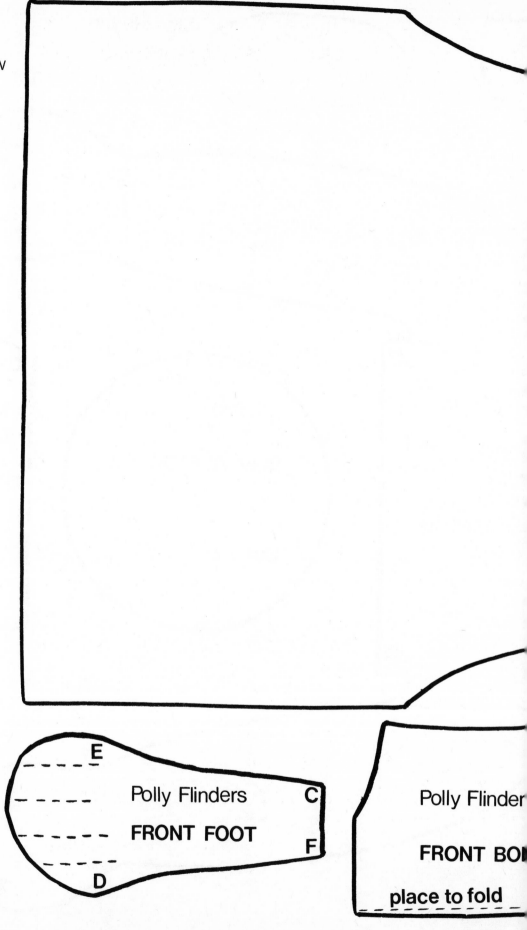

E

Polly Flinders

C

FRONT FOOT

F

D

Polly Flinder

FRONT BO

place to fold

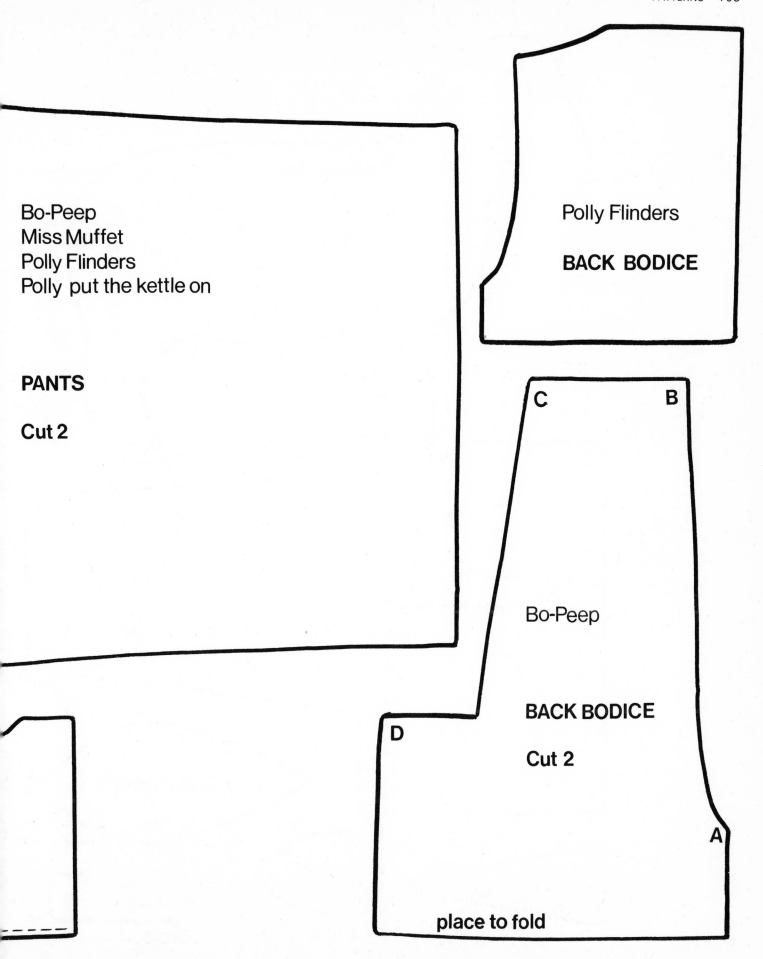

Polly Flinders

BACK BODICE

Bo-Peep
Miss Muffet
Polly Flinders
Polly put the kettle on

PANTS

Cut 2

C B

Bo-Peep

BACK BODICE

D

Cut 2

A

place to fold

LITTLE BO-PEEP

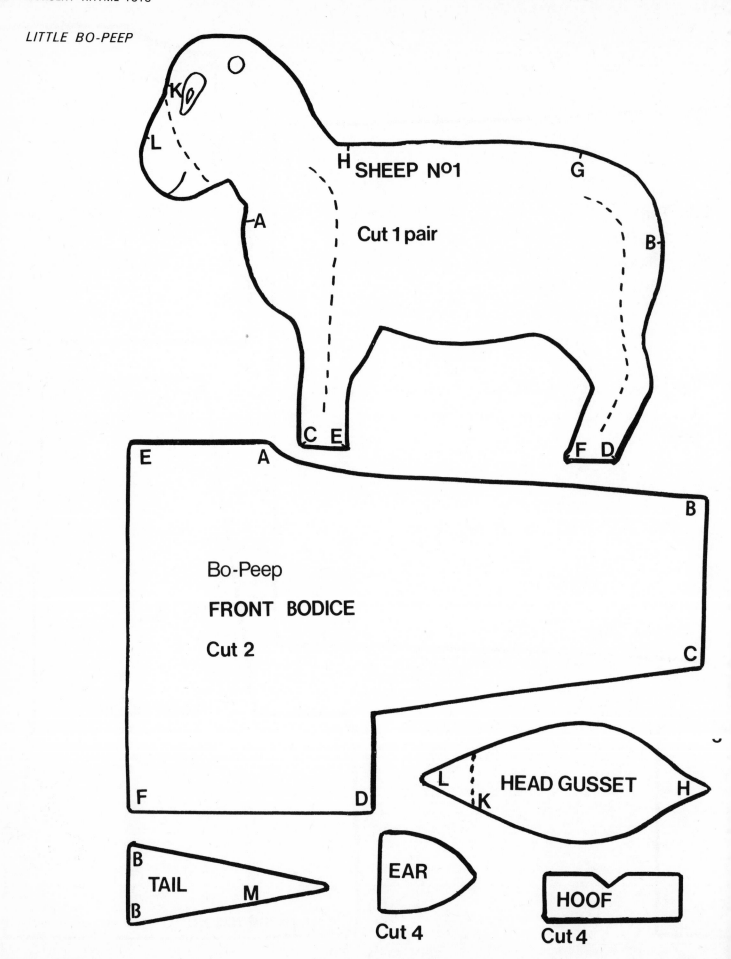

SHEEP Nº1

Cut 1 pair

Bo-Peep

FRONT BODICE

Cut 2

HEAD GUSSET

TAIL

EAR

Cut 4

HOOF

Cut 4

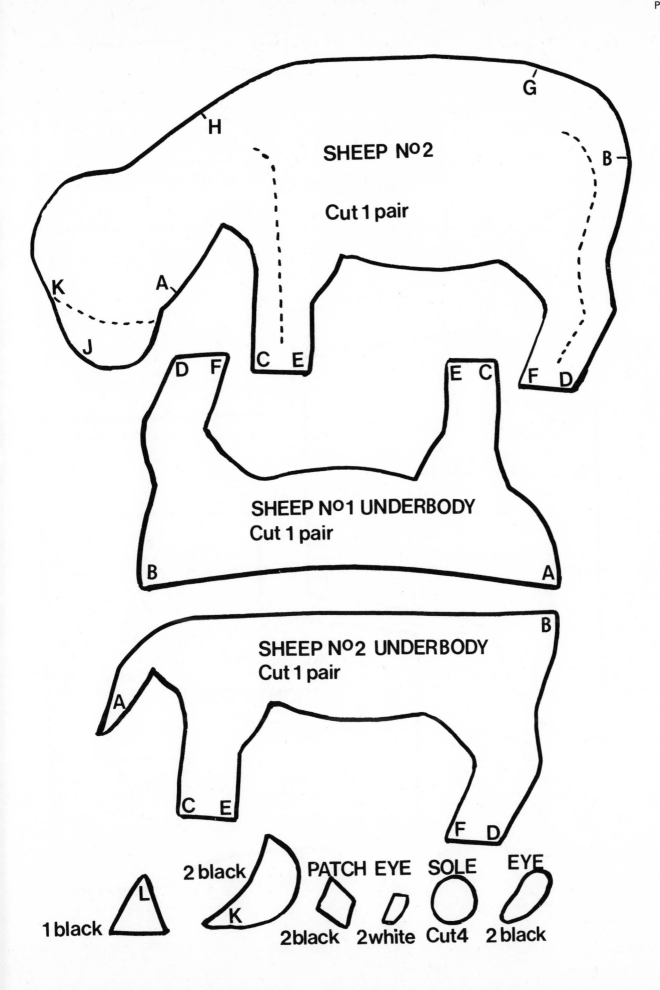

SHEEP Nº 2

Cut 1 pair

SHEEP Nº 1 UNDERBODY
Cut 1 pair

SHEEP Nº 2 UNDERBODY
Cut 1 pair

1 black

2 black

PATCH EYE

2black   2white

SOLE

Cut 4

EYE

2 black

LITTLE MISS MUFFET
LITTLE POLLY FLINDERS
POLLY PUT THE KETTLE ON

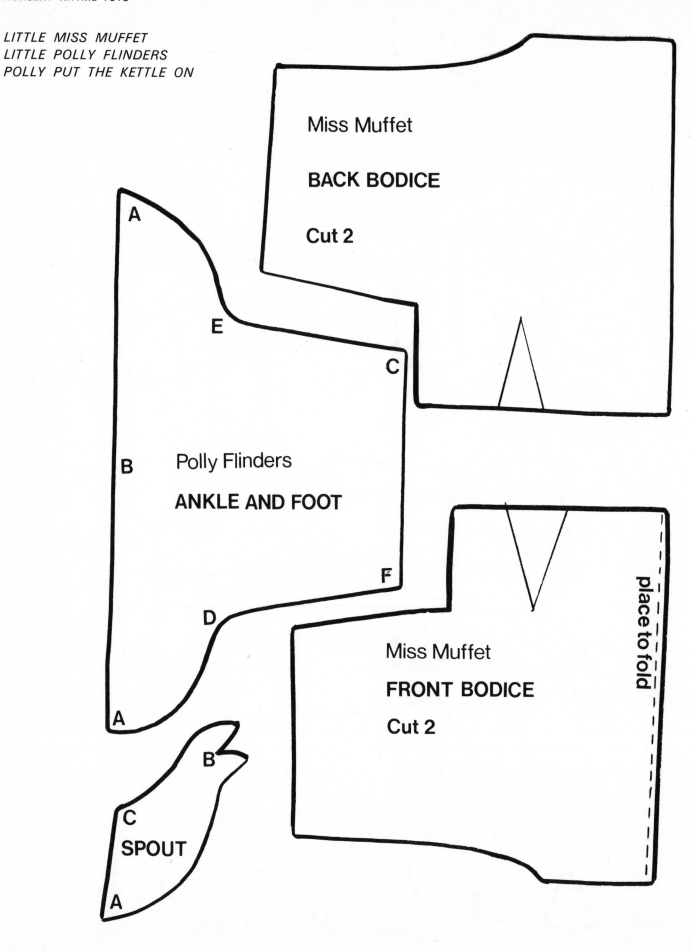

Miss Muffet

BACK BODICE

Cut 2

A

E

C

B

Polly Flinders

ANKLE AND FOOT

F

D

A

B

C

SPOUT

A

Miss Muffet

FRONT BODICE

Cut 2

place to fold

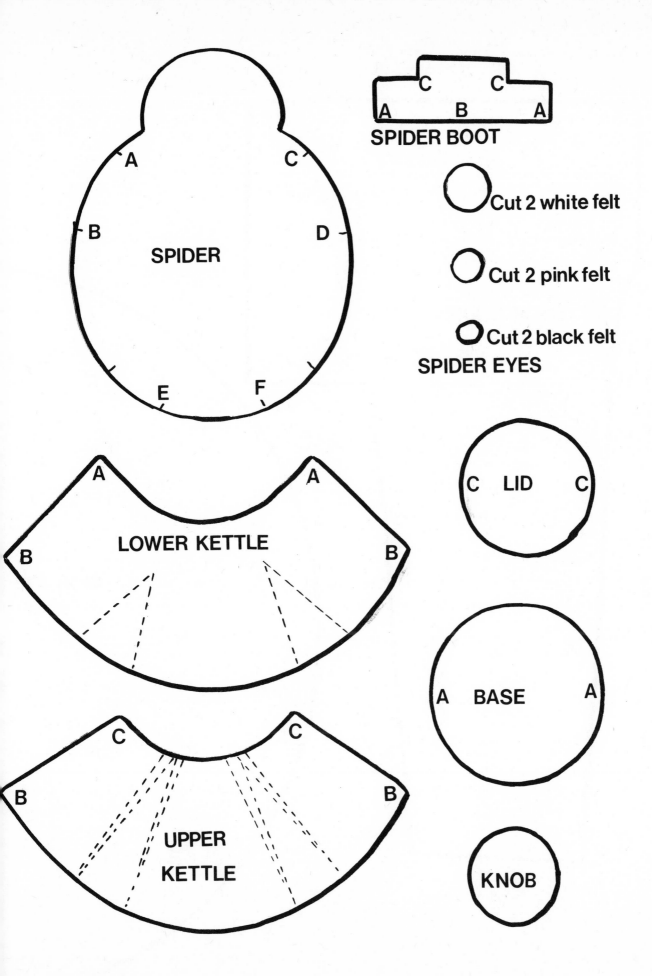

SPIDER BOOT

SPIDER

Cut 2 white felt

Cut 2 pink felt

Cut 2 black felt

SPIDER EYES

LOWER KETTLE

LID

UPPER

KETTLE

BASE

KNOB

POLLY PUT THE KETTLE ON

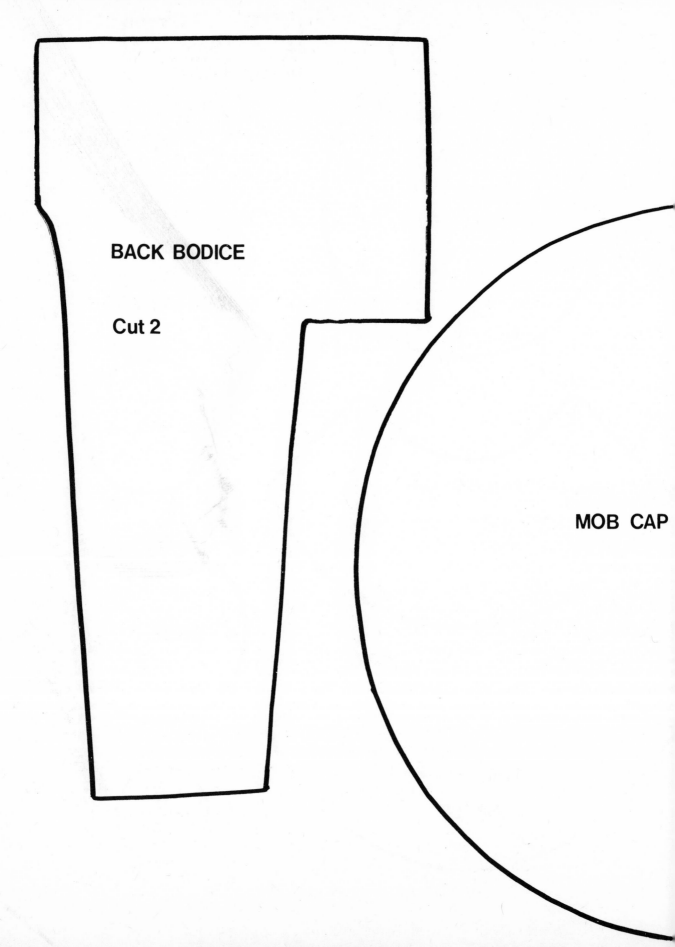

BACK BODICE

Cut 2

MOB CAP

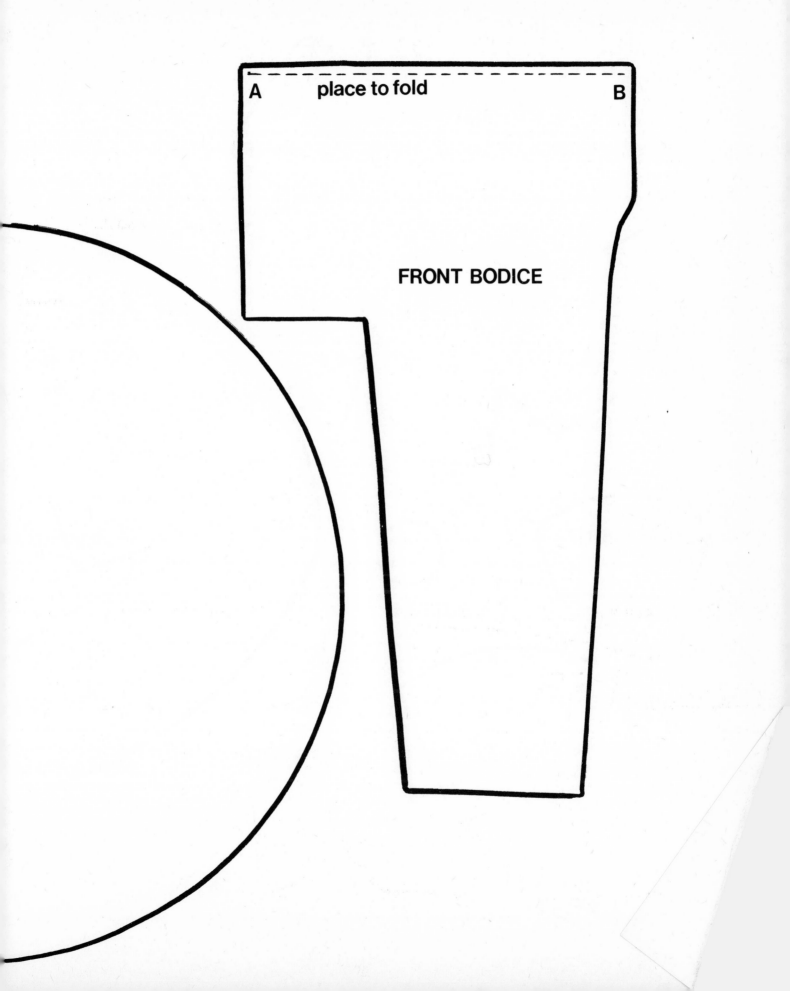

A place to fold B

FRONT BODICE

LITTLE JACK HORNER

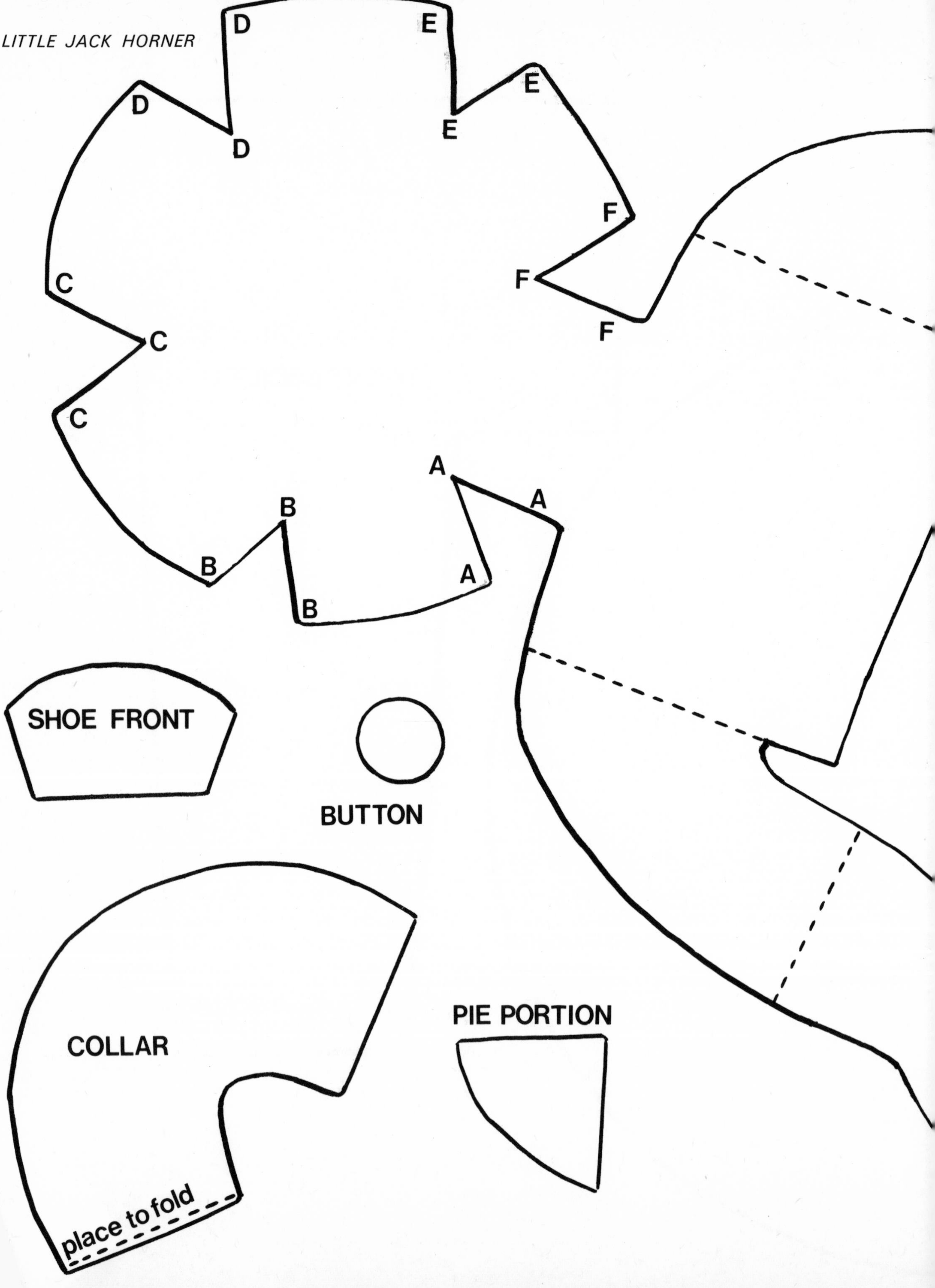

D

E

D

D

D

E

E

E

F

F

F

C

C

C

A

A

B

B

A

B

SHOE FRONT

BUTTON

COLLAR

PIE PORTION

place to fold

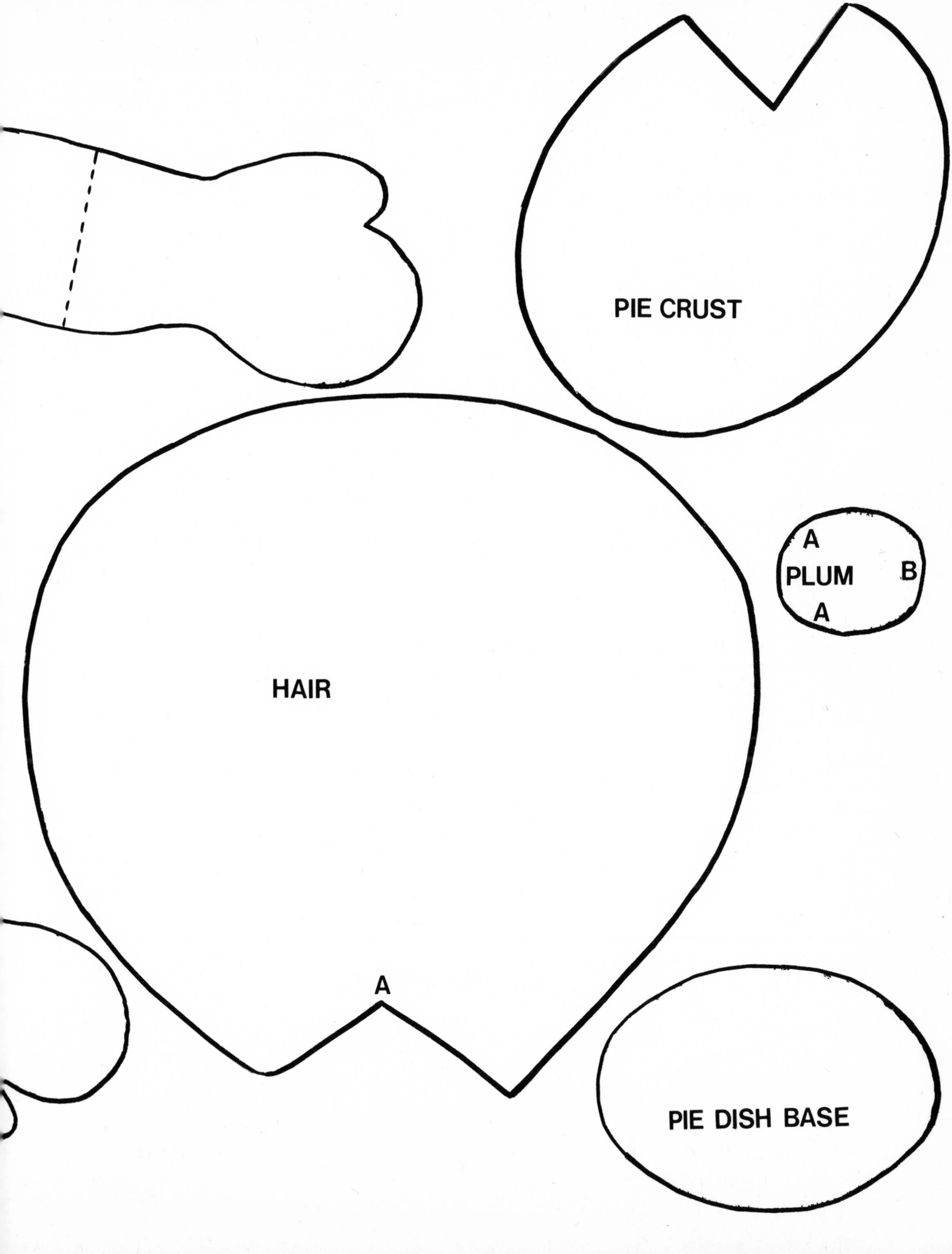

PIE CRUST

PLUM

A

B

A

HAIR

A

PIE DISH BASE

LITTLE JACK HORNER

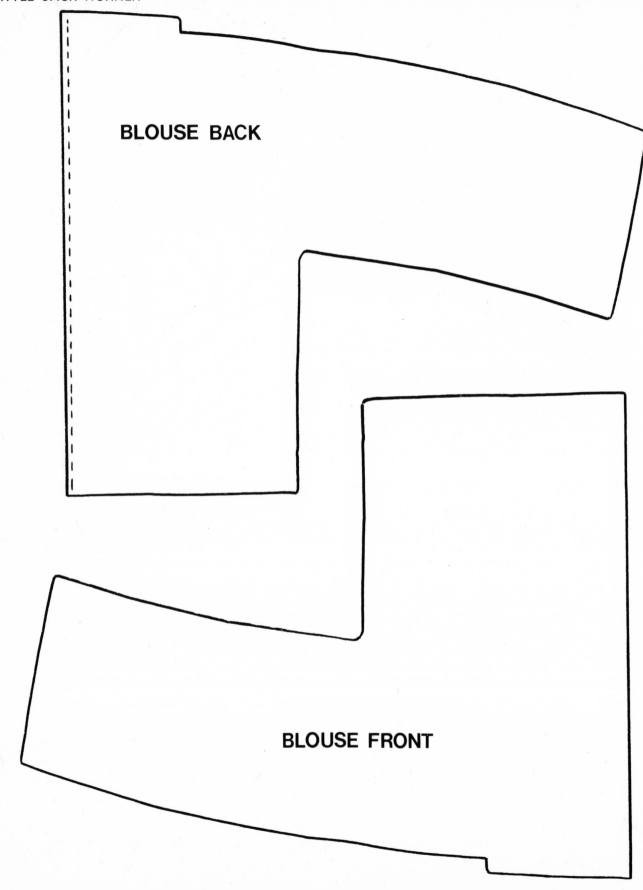

BLOUSE BACK

BLOUSE FRONT

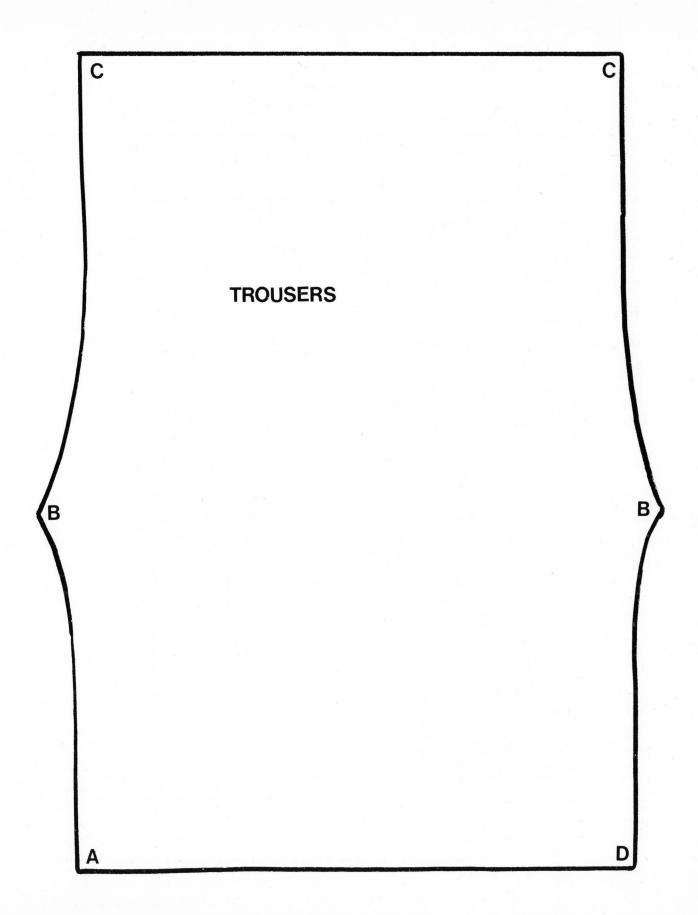

TROUSERS

LITTLE JACK HORNER

A

C

SOCK

D   D

BODY AND LEGS

C

C

A

BUCKLE

PIE DISH
SIDES

E

SOLE

G   G

F

A   D   A

SHOE UPPER

F

E   E

LITTLE BOY BLUE

WAISTBAND Cut 2

HORN

X

DUNGAREES

A

C

Cut 2

D

B

BIB

fold

Cut 1

waist

A B

STRAP Cut 2

A B

RIDE A COCK HORSE
LITTLE BOY BLUE

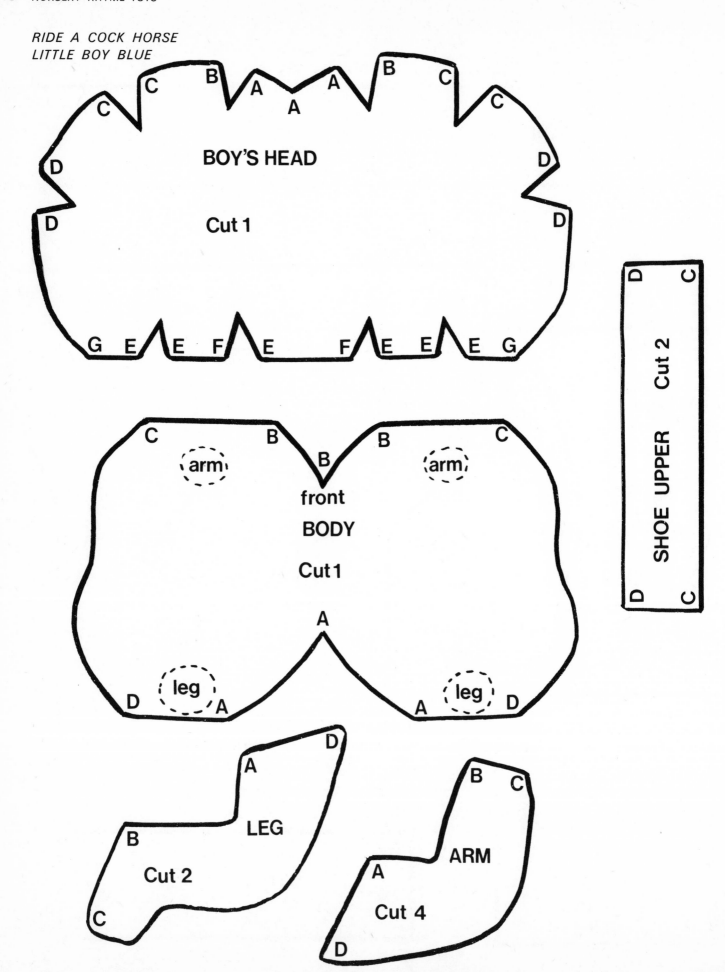

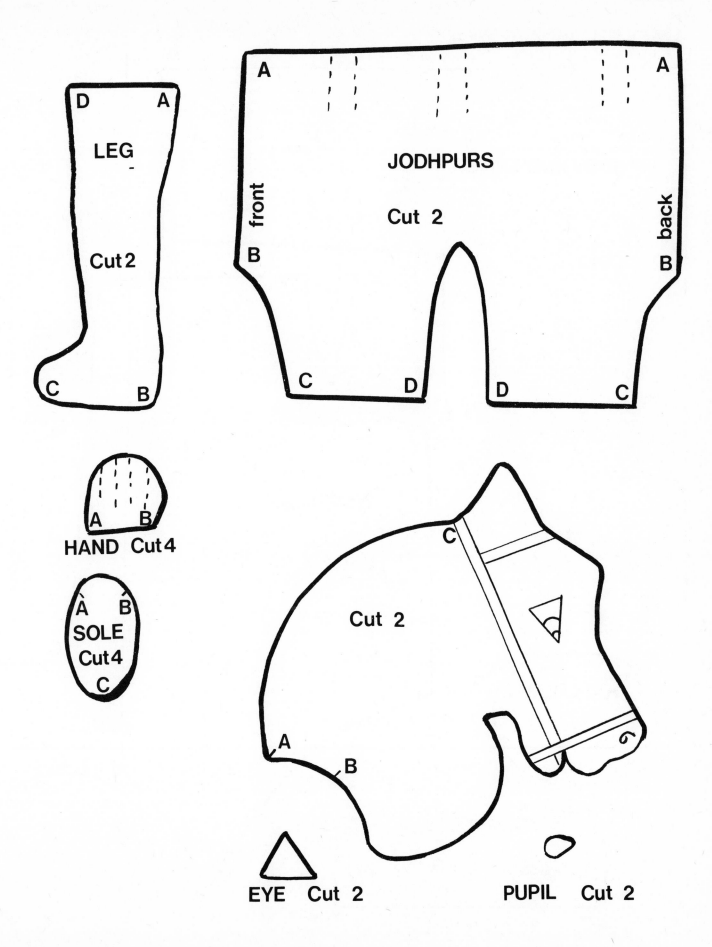

LEG Cut 2

JODHPURS Cut 2

front

back

HAND Cut 4

SOLE Cut 4

Cut 2

EYE Cut 2

PUPIL Cut 2

A FROG HE WOULD A-WOOING GO

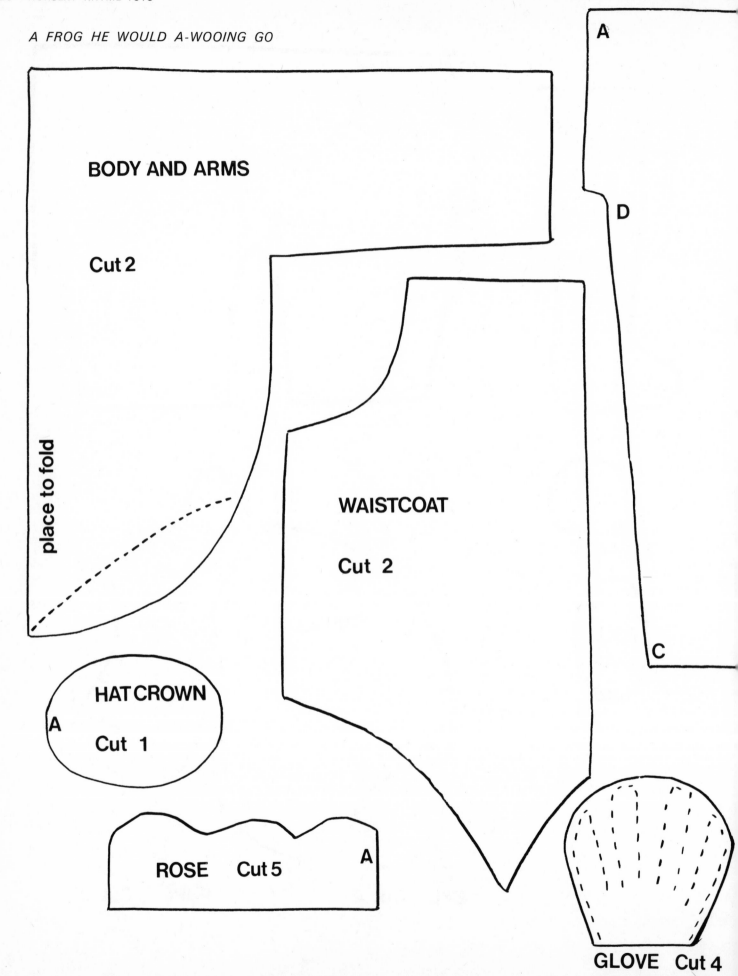

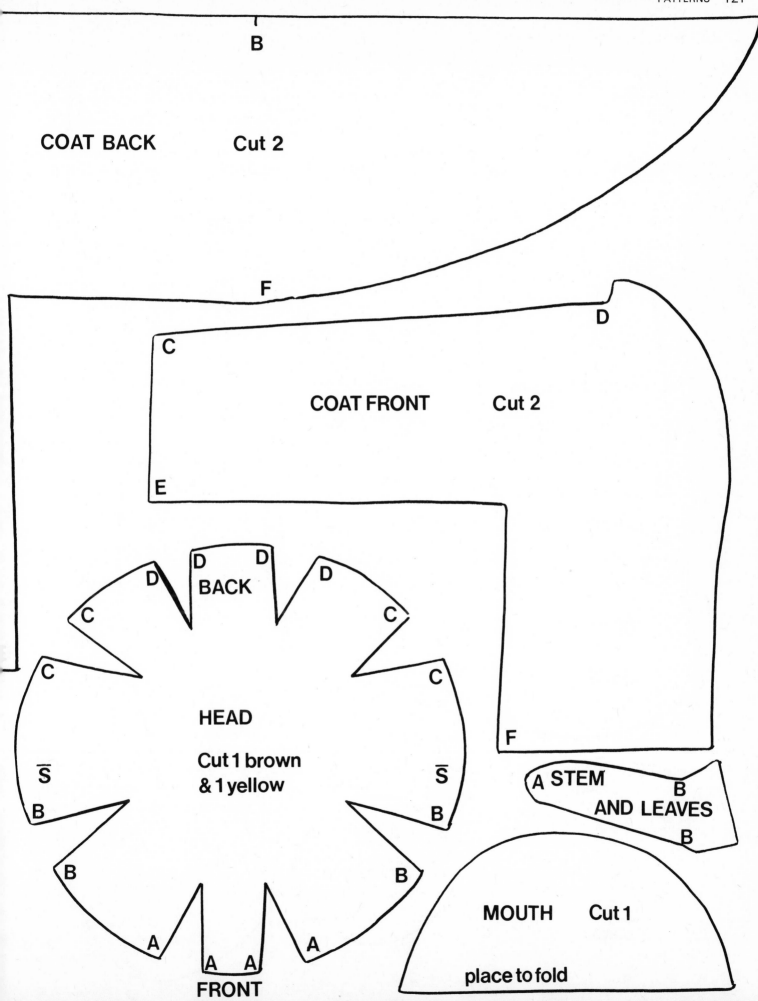

A FROG HE WOULD A-WOOING GO

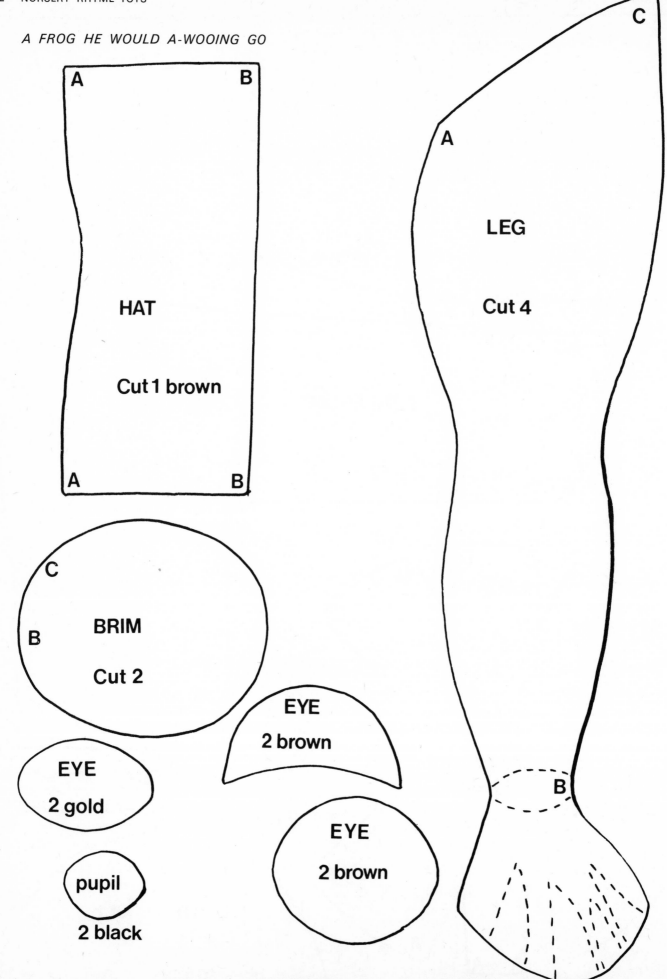

A

B

HAT

Cut 1 brown

A

B

A

LEG

Cut 4

C

C

B

BRIM

Cut 2

EYE

2 brown

EYE

2 gold

B

EYE

2 brown

pupil

2 black

HUMPTY DUMPTY

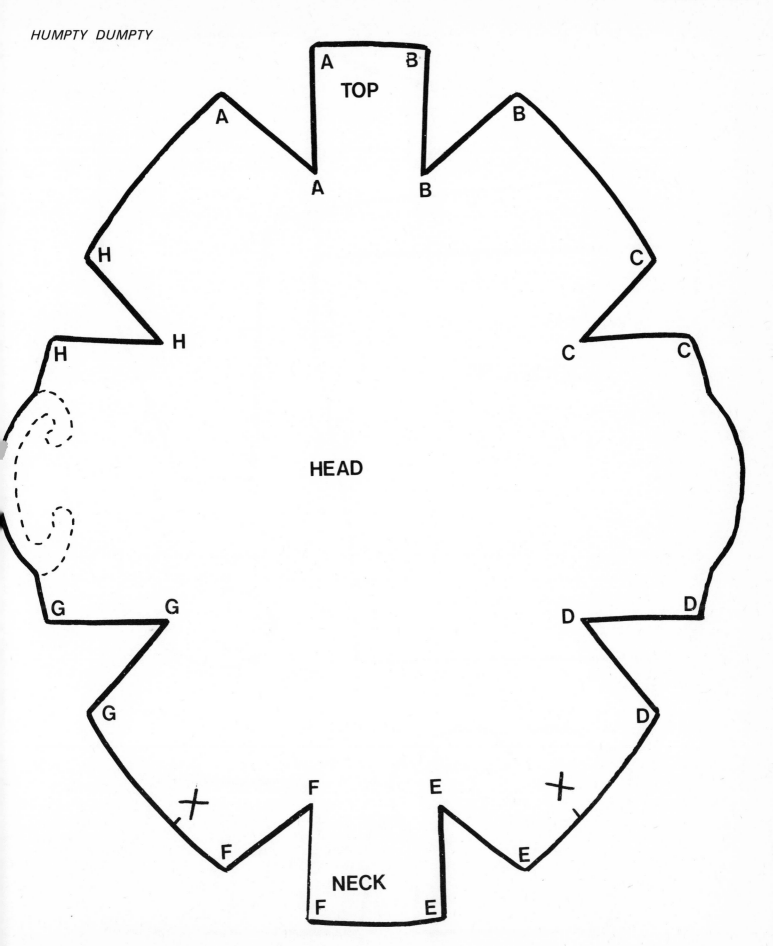

HUMPTY DUMPTY

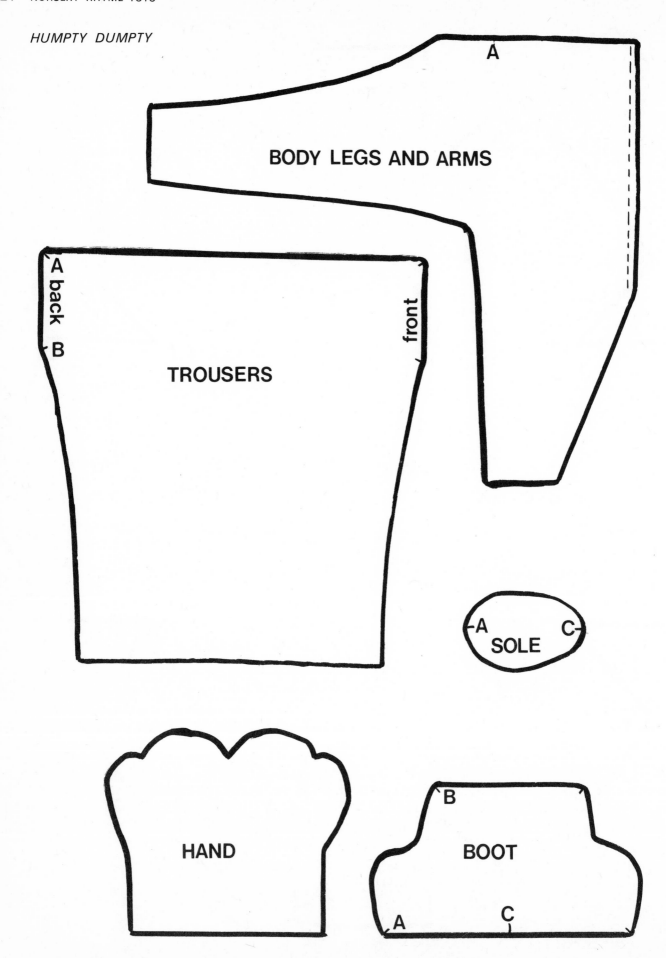

BODY LEGS AND ARMS

A

A
back
B

front

TROUSERS

A SOLE C

HAND

B

BOOT

A   C

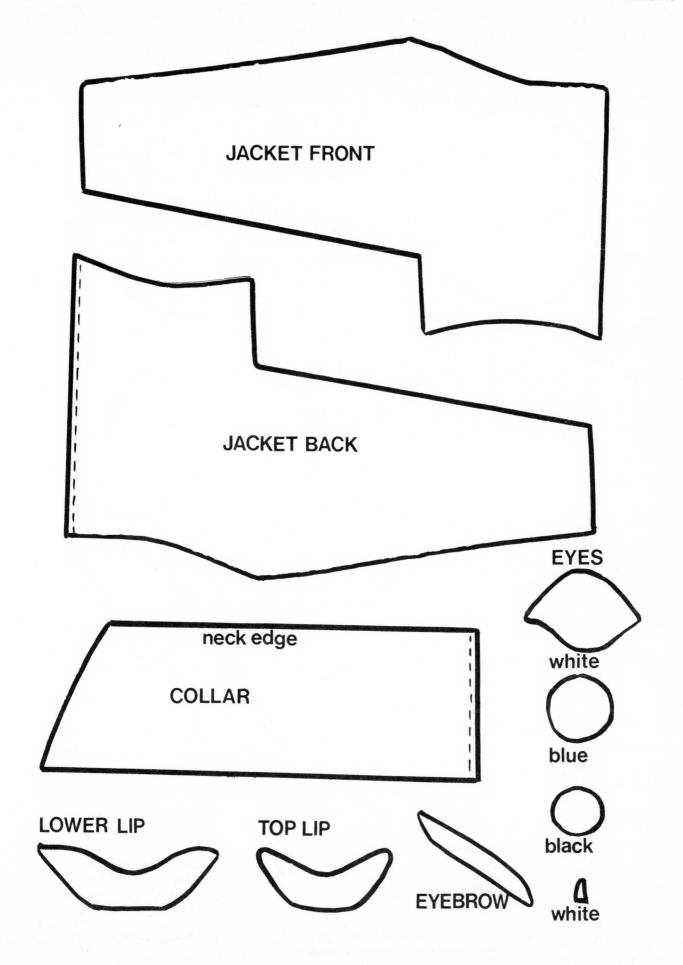

JACKET FRONT

JACKET BACK

EYES

white

blue

black

neck edge

COLLAR

LOWER LIP

TOP LIP

EYEBROW

white

HUMPTY DUMPTY: Guardsman, Cavalry soldier, Queen's (RWSR) Sergeant
Highland soldier
Hussar
Lancer

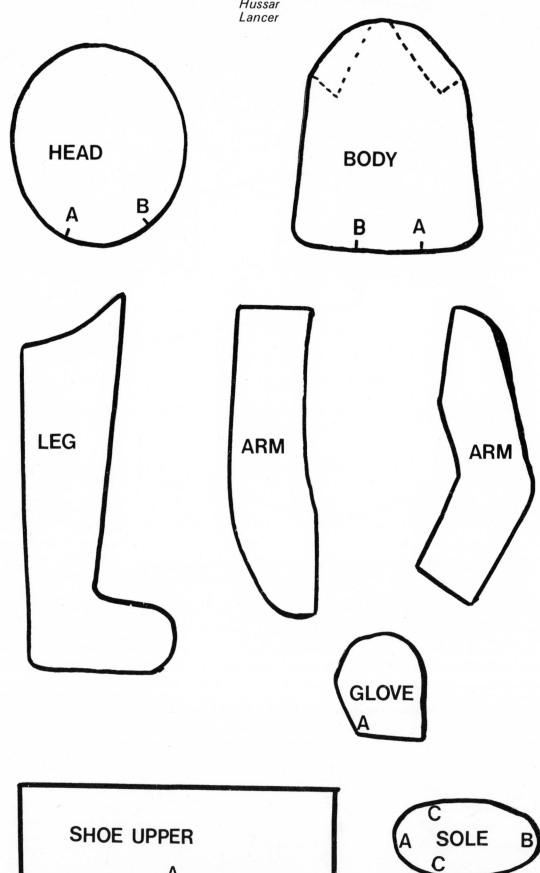

HEAD
A   B

BODY
B   A

LEG

ARM

ARM

GLOVE
A

SHOE UPPER
A

C
A   SOLE   B
C

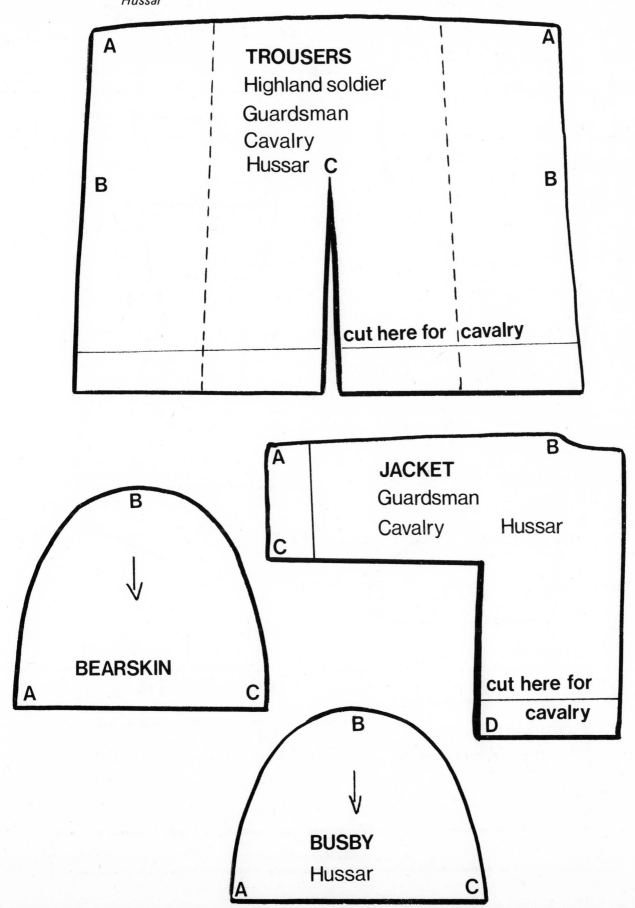

HUMPTY DUMPTY : Guardsman
Highland soldier
Cavalry soldier
Hussar

A

TROUSERS

Highland soldier

Guardsman

Cavalry

B   Hussar   C   B

cut here for cavalry

A

BEARSKIN

A   C

A

C

JACKET

Guardsman

Cavalry   Hussar

B

cut here for

cavalry

D

B

BUSBY

Hussar

A   C

HUMPTY DUMPTY : Cavalry soldier

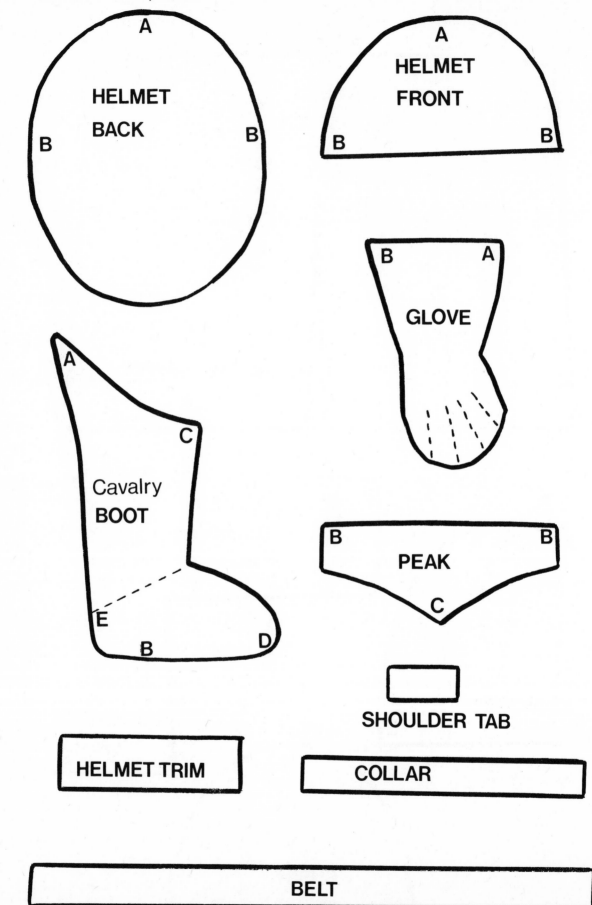

HUMPTY DUMPTY : Highland soldier
Lancer

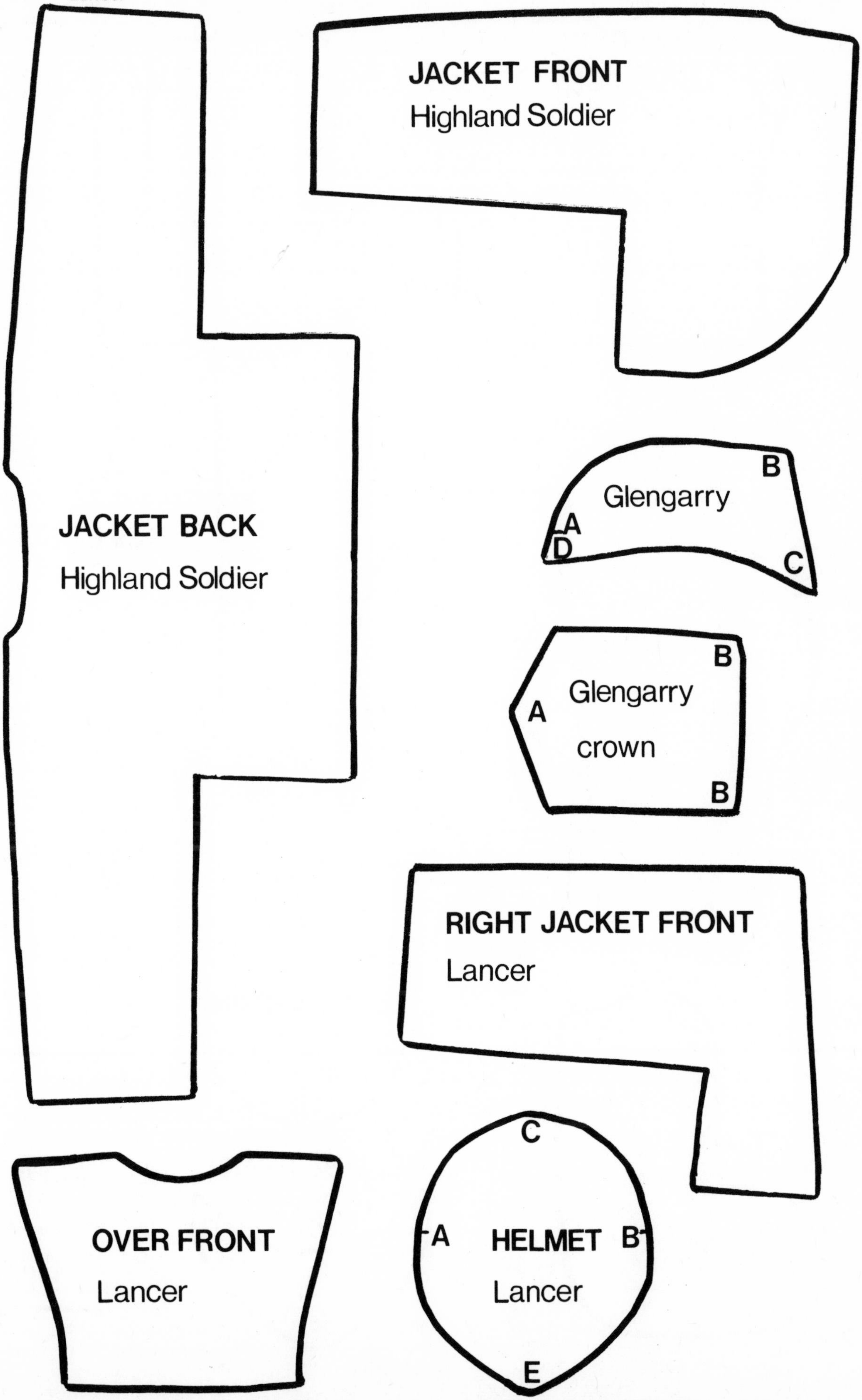

JACKET FRONT
Highland Soldier

JACKET BACK
Highland Soldier

Glengarry

B

A
D

C

Glengarry

crown

B

A

B

RIGHT JACKET FRONT
Lancer

OVER FRONT
Lancer

C

A

HELMET
Lancer

B

E

HUMPTY DUMPTY : Lancer

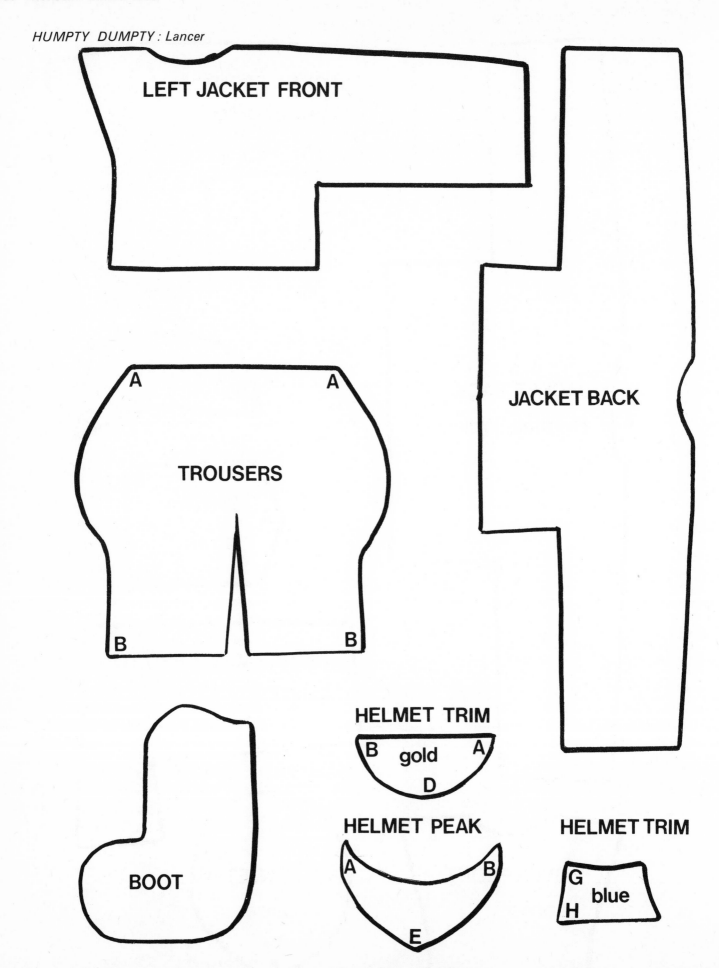

LEFT JACKET FRONT

JACKET BACK

TROUSERS

A   A

B   B

BOOT

HELMET TRIM

B gold A

D

HELMET PEAK

A   B

E

HELMET TRIM

G blue

H

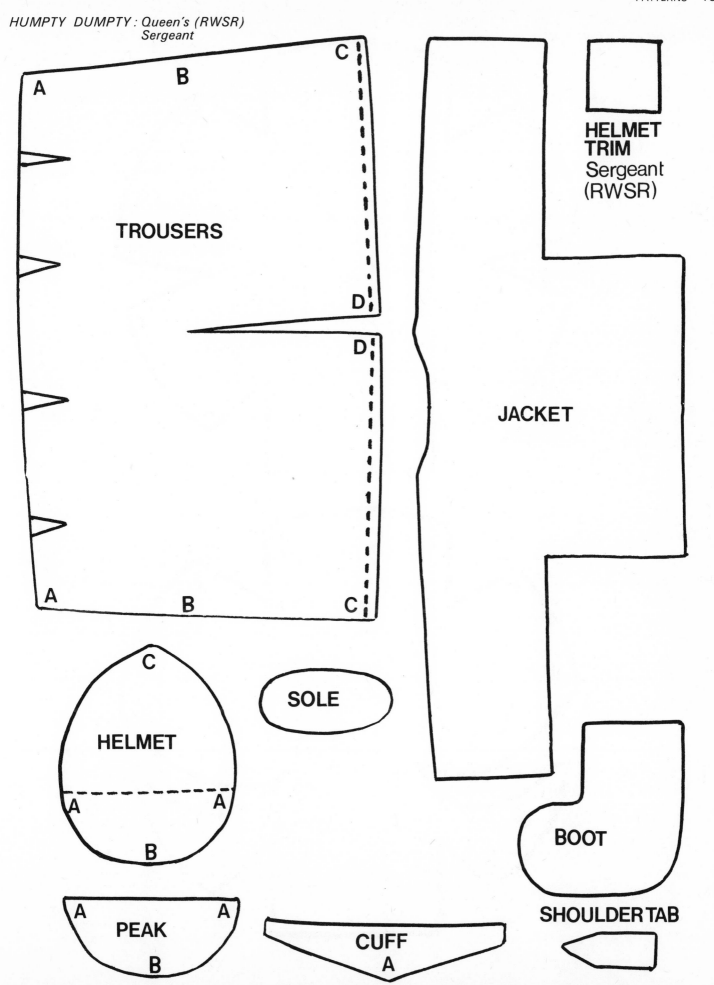

HUMPTY DUMPTY: Queen's (RWSR)
Sergeant

A B C

TROUSERS

D

D

A B C

HELMET TRIM
Sergeant
(RWSR)

JACKET

C

HELMET

A A

B

SOLE

BOOT

A A

PEAK

B

CUFF

A

SHOULDER TAB

SIMPLE SIMON : Pieman

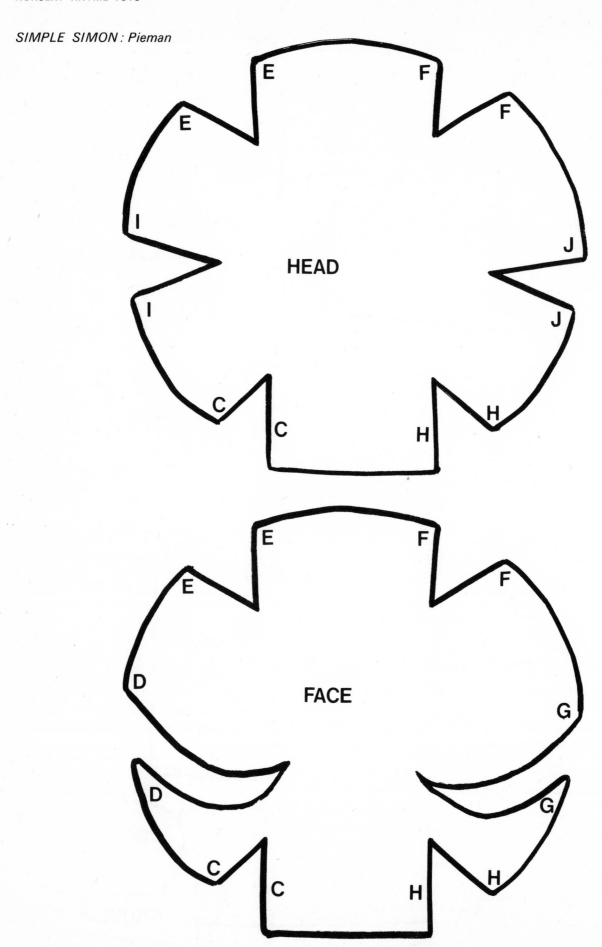

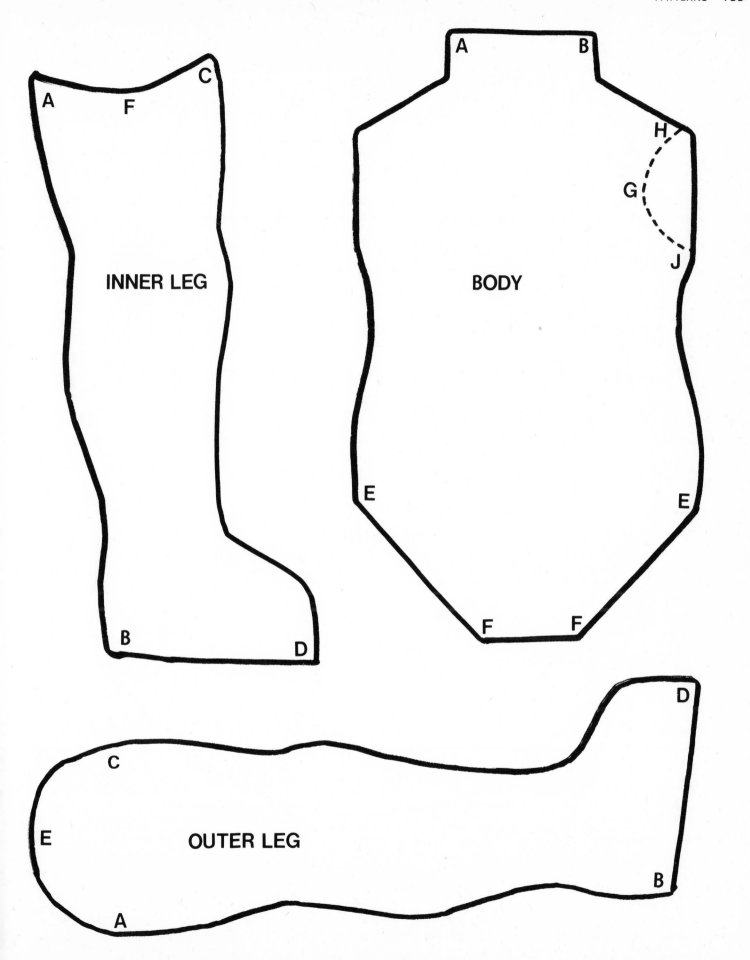

SIMPLE SIMON
YANKEE DOODLE

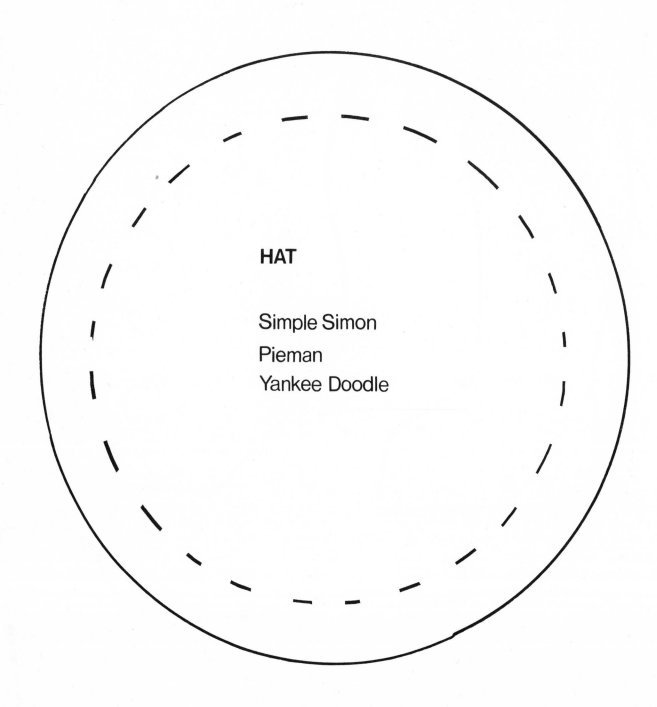

HAT

Simple Simon

Pieman

Yankee Doodle

SIMPLE SIMON : Pieman

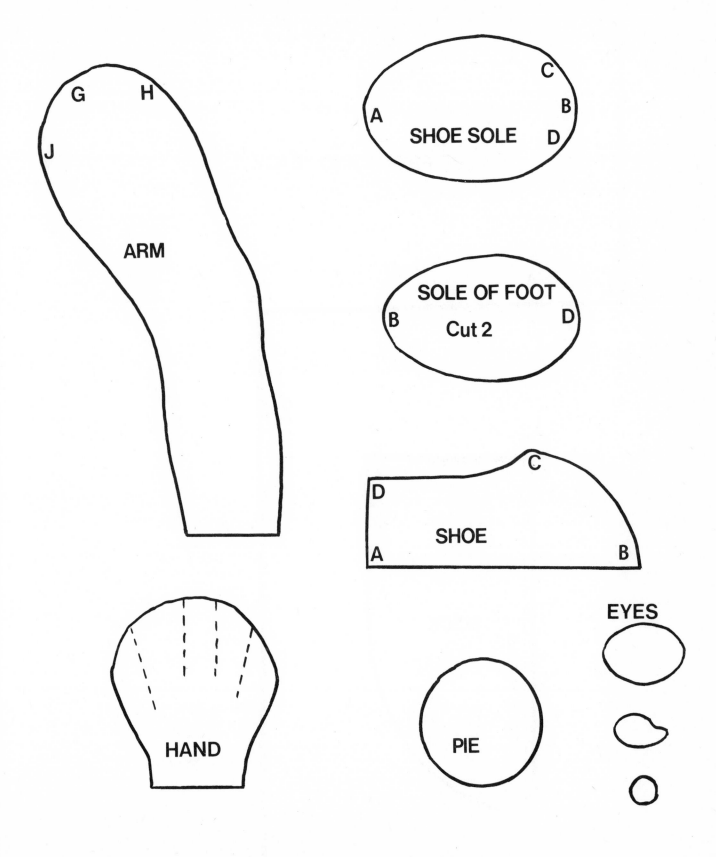

G   H

J

ARM

SHOE SOLE

A   C   B   D

SOLE OF FOOT

Cut 2

B   D

SHOE

D   C   A   B

HAND

PIE

EYES

SIMPLE SIMON : Pieman

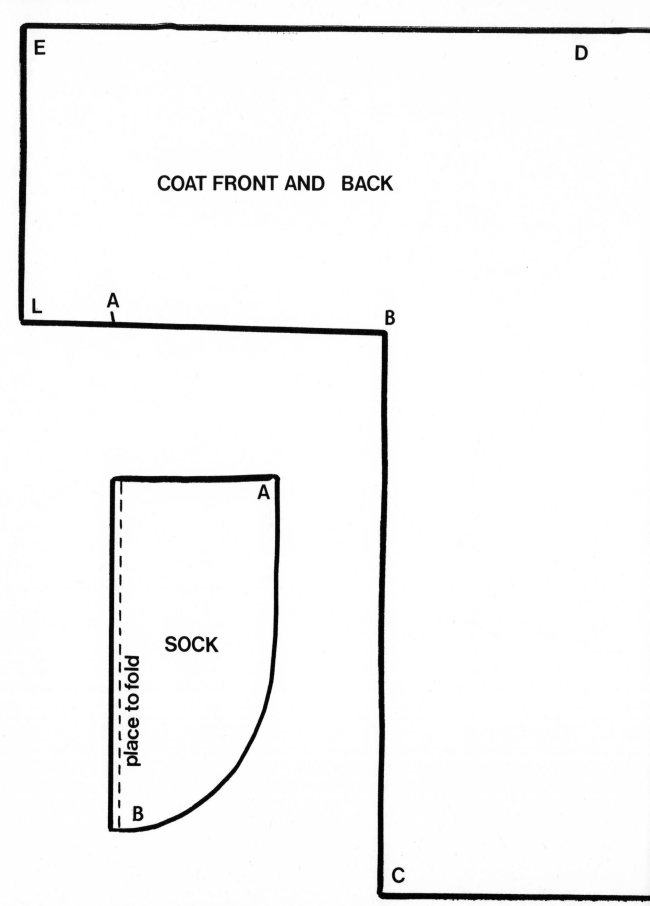

E

D

COAT FRONT AND   BACK

L   A   B

A

SOCK

place to fold

B

C

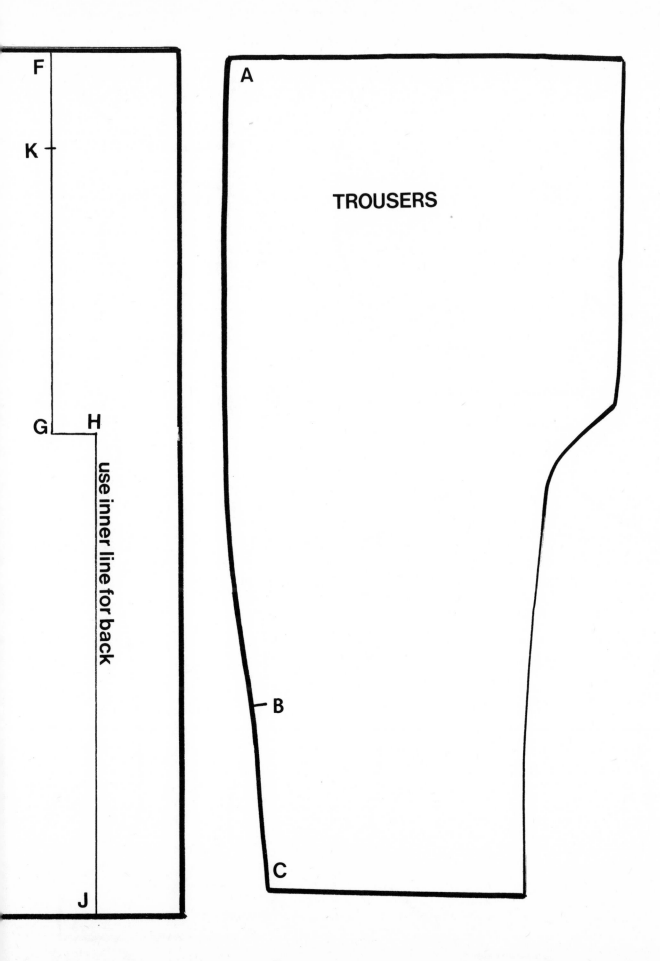

F

K

G H

use inner line for back

J

A

TROUSERS

B

C

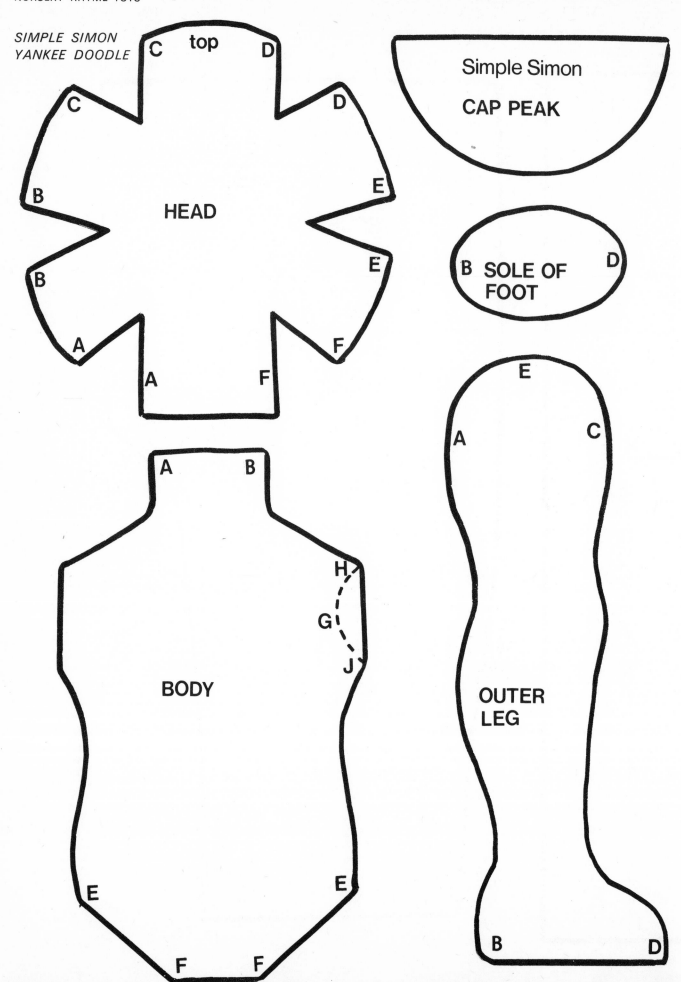

top

HEAD

Simple Simon

CAP PEAK

SOLE OF FOOT

BODY

OUTER LEG

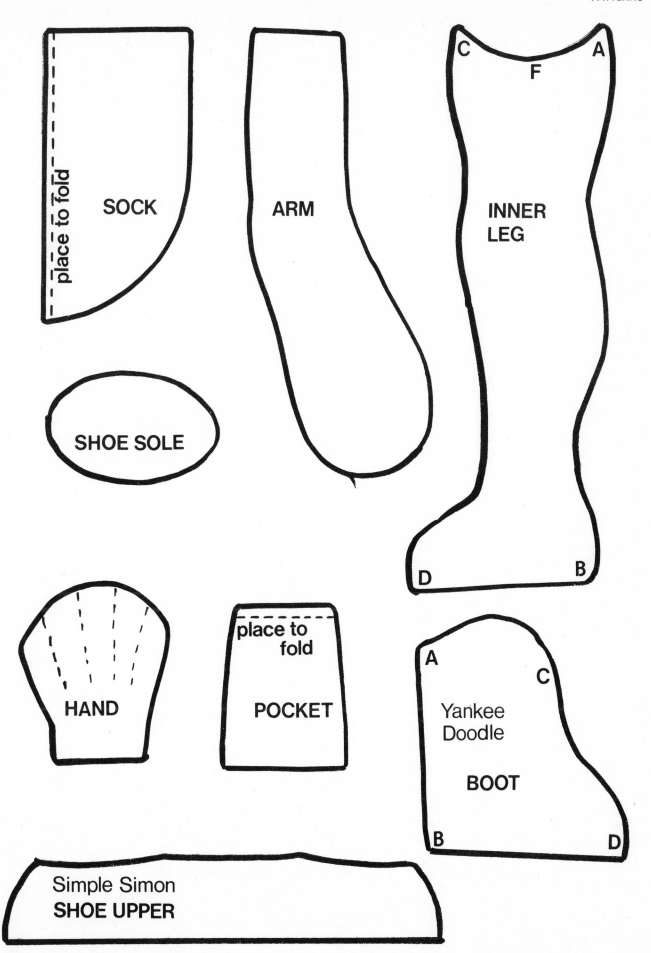

place to fold

SOCK

ARM

C   A
F

INNER
LEG

SHOE SOLE

D   B

HAND

place to
fold

POCKET

A   C

Yankee
Doodle

BOOT

B   D

Simple Simon
SHOE UPPER

SIMPLE SIMON

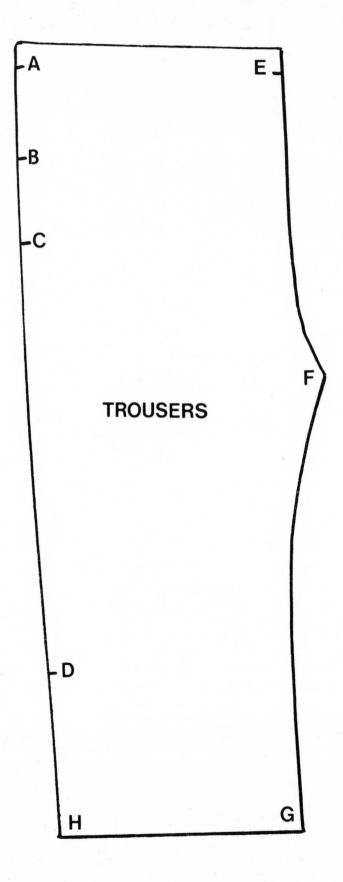

TROUSERS

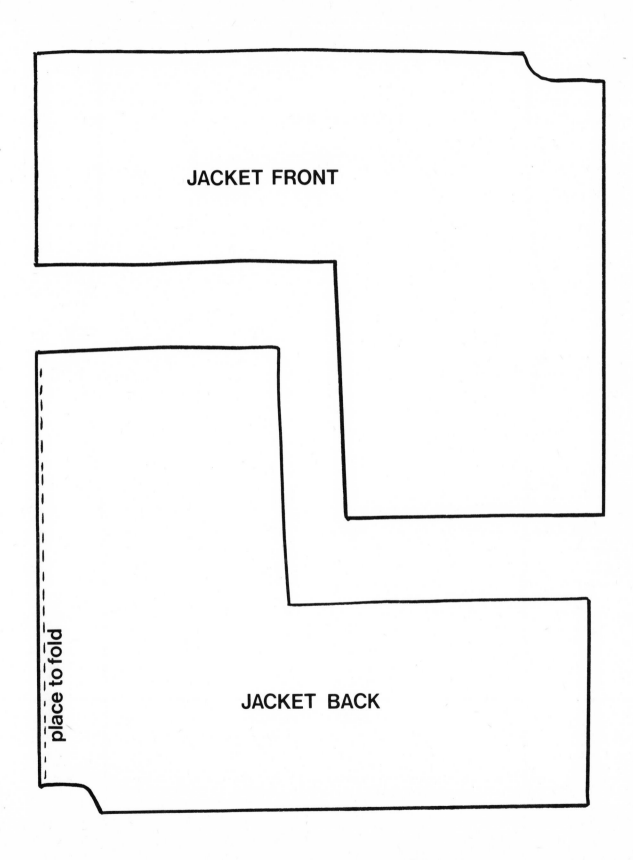

JACKET FRONT

JACKET BACK

place to fold

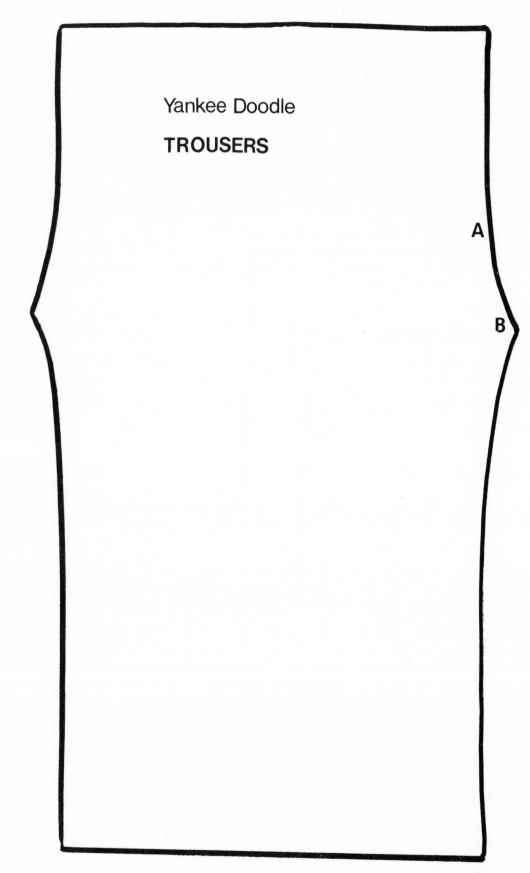

Yankee Doodle

TROUSERS

A

B

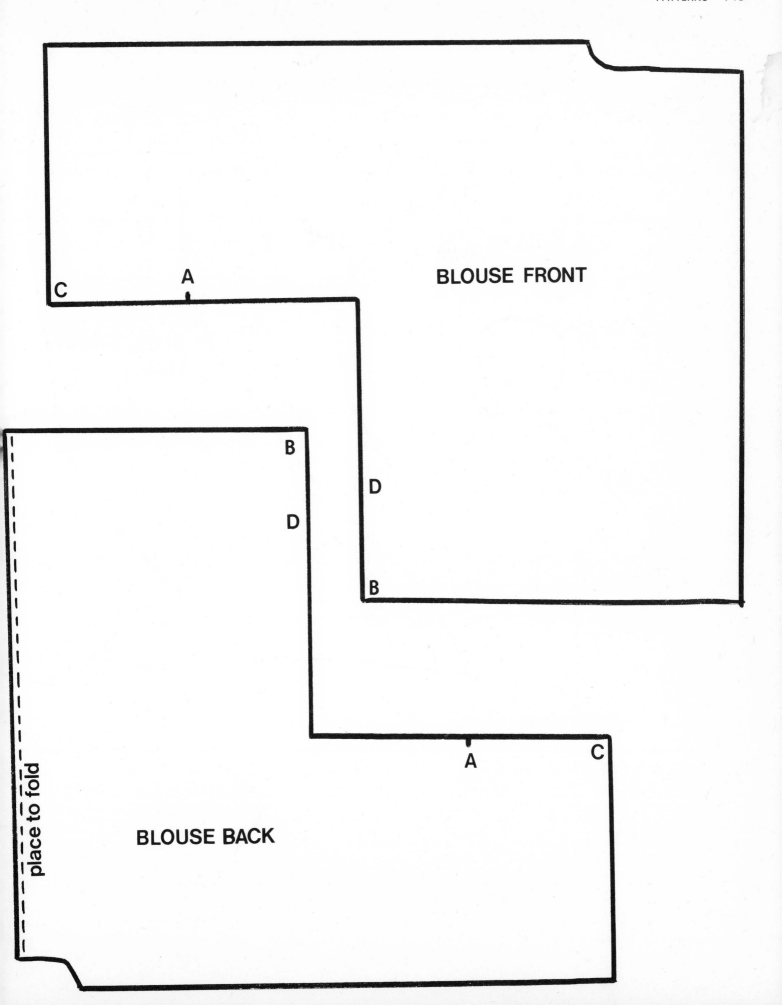

C A   BLOUSE FRONT

B

D   D

D

B

BLOUSE BACK   A   C

place to fold

SIMPLE SIMON
YANKEE DOODLE

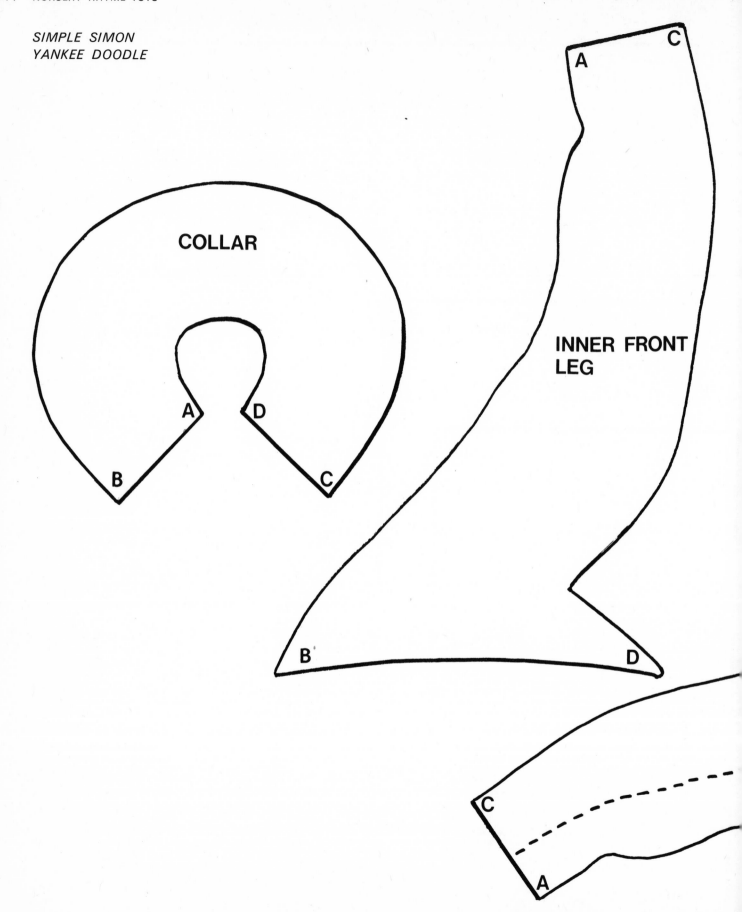

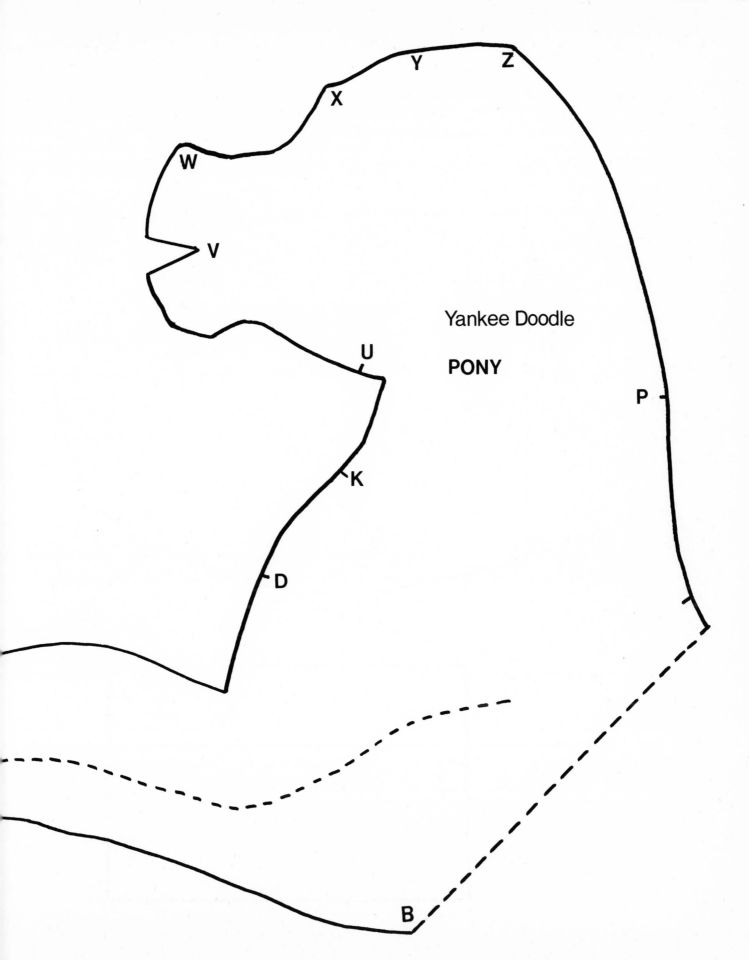

Yankee Doodle

PONY

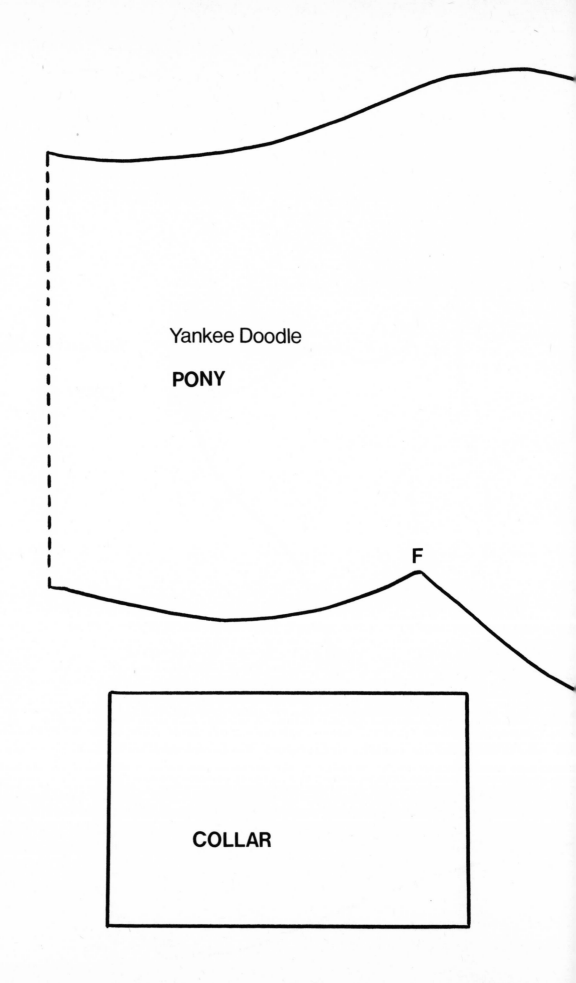

Yankee Doodle

PONY

F

COLLAR

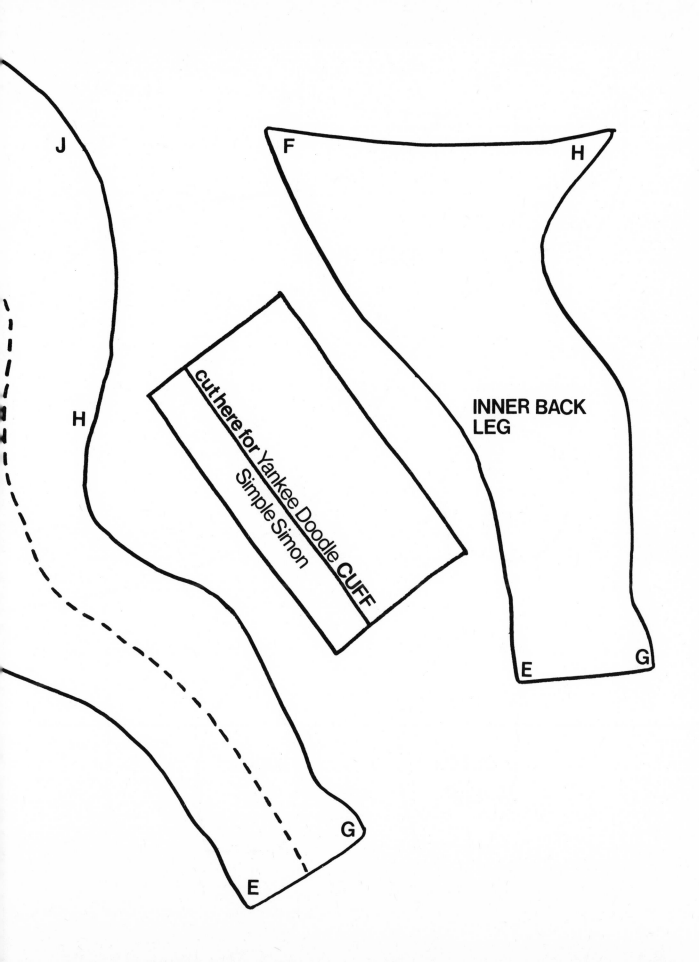

J

F

H

H

INNER BACK
LEG

cut here for Yankee Doodle **CUFF**

Simple Simon

G

E

E

G

YANKEE DOODLE : Pony

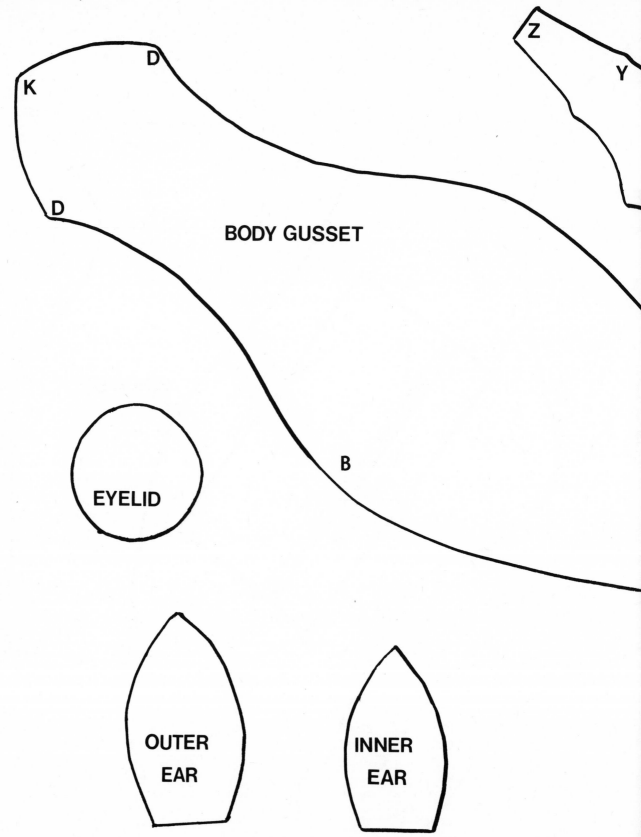

K

D

D

Z

Y

BODY GUSSET

B

EYELID

OUTER EAR

INNER EAR

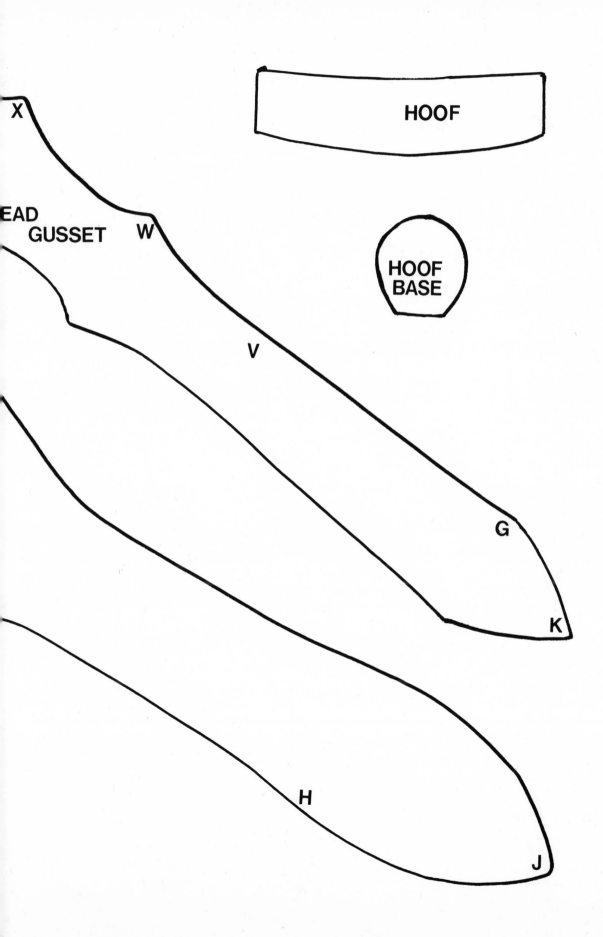

HOOF

HOOF
BASE

X

EAD
GUSSET

W

V

G

K

H

J

JACK AND JILL

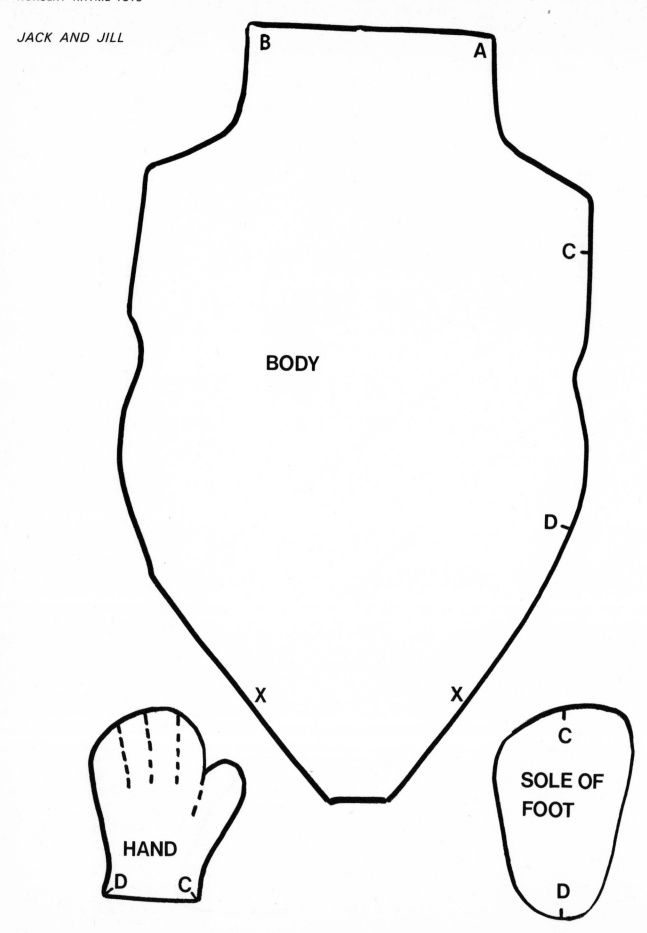

BODY

HAND

SOLE OF FOOT

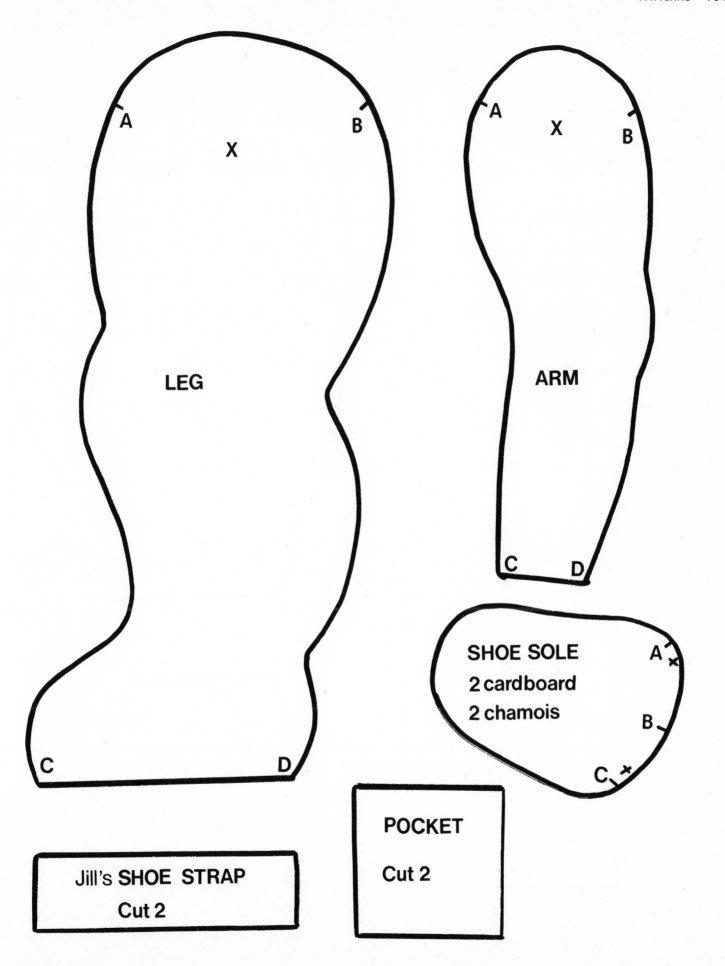

A

B

X

A

X

B

LEG

ARM

C

D

C

D

SHOE SOLE

2 cardboard

2 chamois

A

B

C

C

D

POCKET

Cut 2

Jill's **SHOE STRAP**

Cut 2

JACK AND JILL

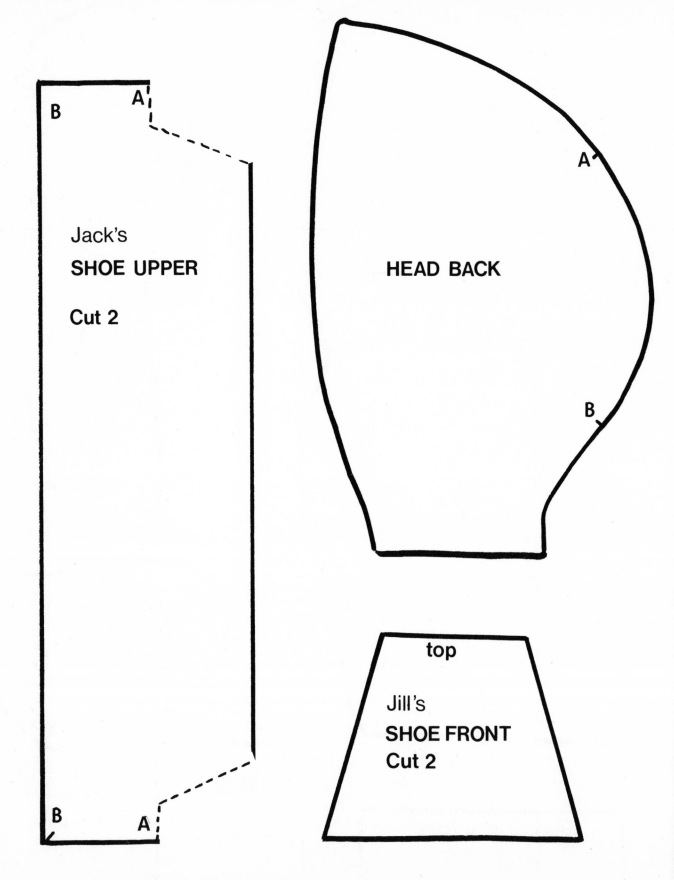

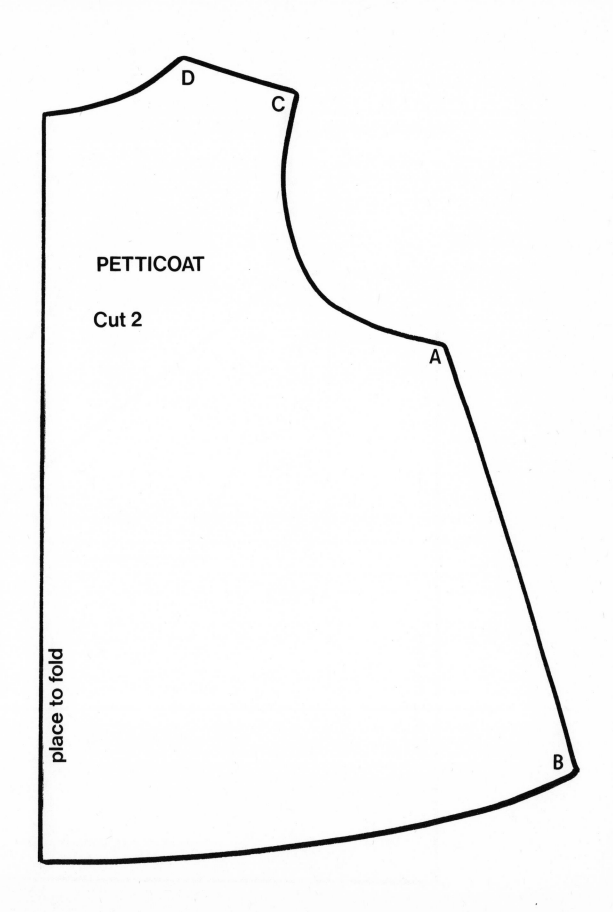

PETTICOAT

Cut 2

place to fold

D

C

A

B

JACK AND JILL : Jack's Jacket

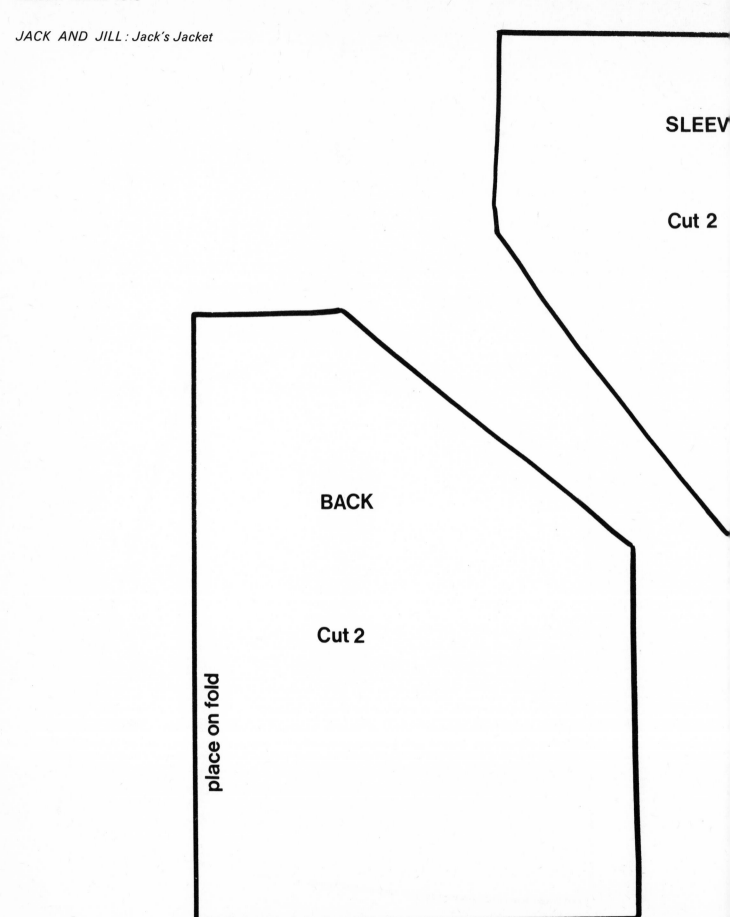

SLEEV

Cut 2

BACK

Cut 2

place on fold

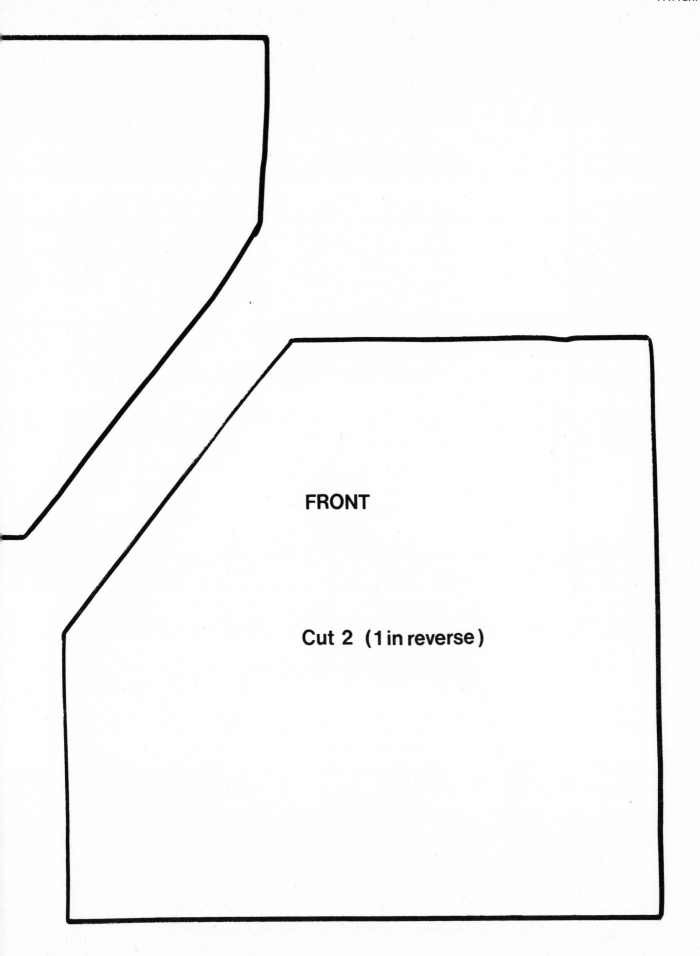

FRONT

Cut 2 (1 in reverse)

JACK AND JILL

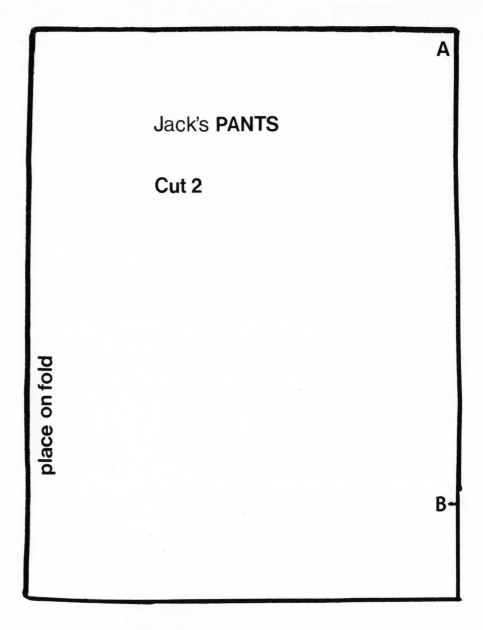

Jack's **PANTS**

Cut 2

place on fold

A

B →

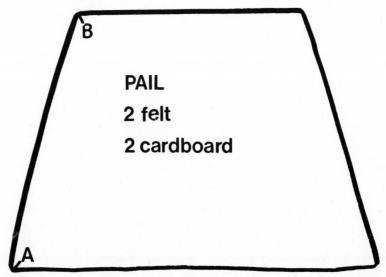

B

PAIL
2 felt
2 cardboard

A

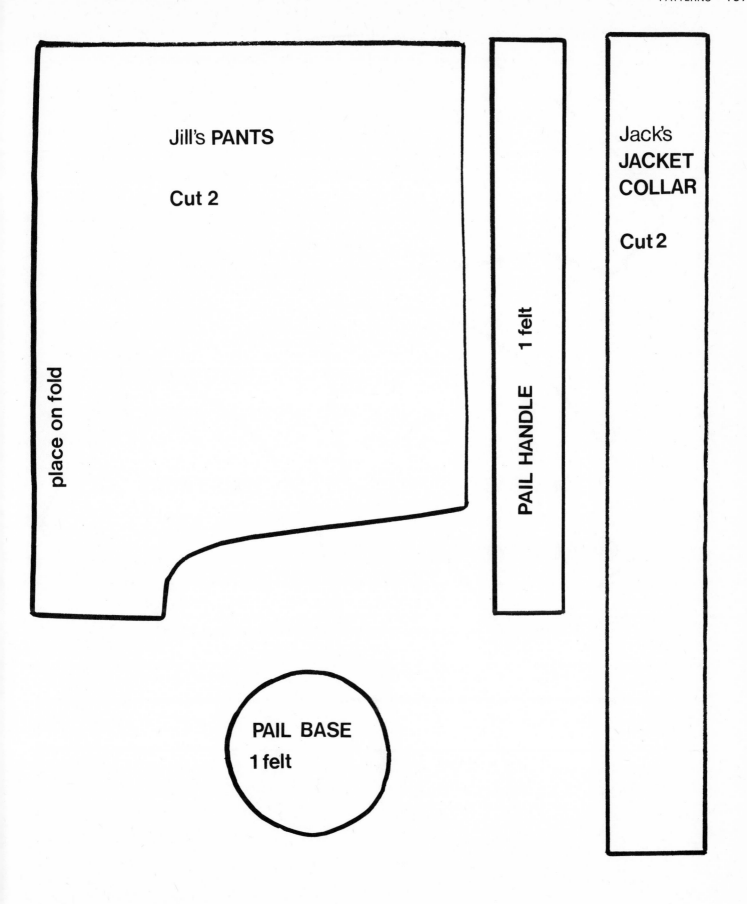

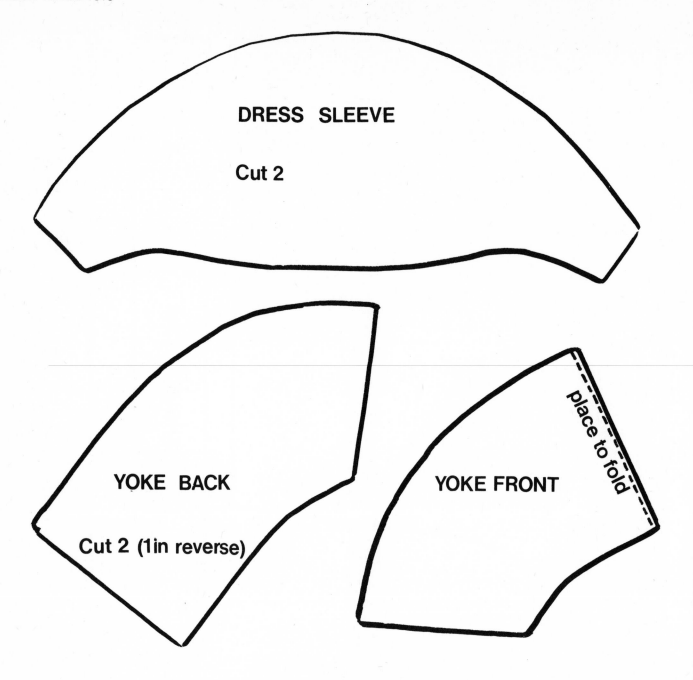

DRESS SLEEVE

Cut 2

YOKE BACK

Cut 2 (1in reverse)

YOKE FRONT

place to fold

G

F

Jill's **SHOE UPPER**

Cut 2

G

F

Jill's **DRESS SKIRT**

Cut 2

place to fold